LYING ON THE BRIDGE

ALSO BY ESTHER COHEN

Ebony Music – Choice
A piano course in 24 volumes

Sweet Suite
Seven songs for piano

Red Riding Hood
A retelling in verse, illustrated by Abigail Elwell-Sutton

LYING ON THE BRIDGE
Glimpses of Childhood

Esther Cohen

EBONY MUSIC & BOOKS

First published in Great Britain in 2016 by

Ebony Music & Books
2 Oakley Drive
GLASGOW
G44 3PY

www.ebonymusic.co.uk

Printed in Glasgow, Scotland
by Bell & Bain Ltd.

A CIP catalogue record for this book
is available from the British Library

ISBN 978-0-9935476-0-7

To Christopher, Timothy, Miriam and Lewis,
who delighted me with their version of
the Monty Python sketch, *The Four Yorkshireman*,
based on my tales.

If you don't recount your family history,
it will be lost. Honor your own stories
and tell them too. The tales may not seem
very important, but they are what binds families
and makes each of us who we are.

Madeleine L'Engle

Eli and Olive Cohen
Their engagement picture before their marriage in 1940

Are you sitting comfortably?

A jumble of postage stamps all over the floor makes a splendid display! So splendid that I have retained the image in my mind for over 60 years. Never were the world's heads of states seen in such a glorious mismatch of juxtaposition as when my brother spread his thousand unsorted postage stamps over the sitting room floor. No doubt, he found that uncovering the carpet beneath was a tedious, painstaking process.

I cannot say that I have found it tedious to recover the stories of my childhood from the carpet of my memory, where they lay all in a muddle, one hiding bits of another. But it has been painstaking – and, sometimes even a bit painful. Perhaps I have not been brave enough to explore some areas of the carpet yet...

My stories are based around the everyday events of childhood. Nothing special really, except to me, as it was *my* life. I hope, though, that there will be some similarities to identify with as well as some differences to be intrigued by.

In an era when most people married in their twenties and had children soon after, my father was 56 when I arrived in 1949. He was born in 1894, shortly after his Jewish family arrived in Manchester from a village in Lithuania. When we studied WWI in school, it was no surprise (nor any pleasure!) to find that I was the only pupil whose father had served in the trenches in France.

My mother was 15 years younger than my father but was

still over 40 when I was born. She was aged six and the oldest of four siblings when her own mother died. As her father was a professional soldier, the oldest three children were sent to an orphanage where my mother lived until she was 16. There she became well versed in all the skills necessary for managing a home, although perhaps less so in those required for managing the people who lived in it. She had been trained TO OBEY and she expected the same of her children. The idea of compromise was not one which either of my parents embraced.

I did not set out to evoke only a wistful reminiscence of life in the 1950s, though perhaps it is not possible to write about such minutiae without inducing nostalgia for the things which might now be seen to symbolise that particular time. I hope that through the stories I have been able to explore one child's growing awareness of herself and to observe how her developing personality unfolded, both in the general setting of that time and in the more particular setting of her family.

My father's distinctiveness did not stop at his age and origins. I will leave the rest to be gleaned from the snippets about him – and my mother – which pepper my stories. Suffice to say that my family was defined by my parents' faith. They lived their faith in every aspect of their lives – from teething to tithing. I am grateful for, and inspired by, their commitment. But I can't deny that the totality of their approach made life difficult for us, their children, in ways which kept us apart from other people. Inevitably, some of my stories are based on the consequences of these restrictions.

I do not wish to belittle my parents' faith. If I mock

anything, it is the unnecessary burdens which were imposed on us and which really had nothing to do with the essence of their faith. It saddens me to think how these little obstacles made it so hard for me to distinguish and hold on to the big truths. It has taken a huge desire and effort of will to see past the strictness of my upbringing and embrace the example of my parents' lives truly lived out in the service of others.

Then I'll begin!

Contents

Bridgeton, Glasgow

age 0–4

Lying on the Bridge

The front windows of our tenement overlooked the River Clyde. My three older brothers were able to play cricket on the greens of Richmond Park and see my mother waving for them to come home for dinner. Just five minutes to race through the park gates, over the Rutherglen Bridge, turn left into Newhall Street and left again into the terrace to our home in Greenhead Street. Just five minutes for my brothers. But *apparently* when they had me with them, it wasn't so straightforward.

Awww, one might coo, you were only four years old. Your wee legs would be sure to slow them down.

True enough, but that wasn't the problem. *Apparently* I didn't use my wee legs. *Apparently*, as soon as we got on that bridge, I would refuse to go any further and would demonstrate my resolve by lying down on the pavement. *Apparently* they couldn't get me up for anything. *Apparently* my oldest brother would be in trouble because we were late for dinner. *Apparently* this happened quite regularly.

So they tell me. But I *know* I would never have done a thing like that.

Christmas myth

I arrived, two days after Christmas 1949, to be the little sister for Paul (7), Stephen (almost 6) and Daniel (3). It seems my mother had this birth malarkey under control by this time. Knowing she was in labour, she got up, cooked bacon and eggs for the family, then retired to the recess bed in the kitchen where I was born in the early afternoon, while the three little boys sat outside the room on the stairs. The new little girl must have put my father in jovial mood; the midwife was tipped beyond his means or her expectation. But the brothers were rather underwhelmed at the appearance of 'ickle sister' (*pace* Daniel) rather than the addition to their squad that they were hoping for.

I cannot corroborate the accuracy of this account of my birth though there is no doubt of my appearance in it. The version of my entrance to the world which my parents told me is one I can relate with much more conviction. I was enchanted by it and repeated it many times to many people – until I began to be aware of the penetrating looks which adults were giving me as I did so.

That tale goes like this: my brothers had hung up their stockings as usual on Christmas Eve and opened them as usual on Christmas morning. Now here's the bit that should have aroused my suspicions. They didn't search to the very bottom of one of the stockings. Guess what they found there two days later?

Honestly! I ask you! What self-respecting boy does not check to the very bottom of his stocking?

Paul, my mother, me (aged 6 months), Daniel, my father, Stephen

Bedtime story

T hey told me that my first bed was the third drawer down in the big chest of drawers in the kitchen. My parents slept in the recess bed in the same room, so it all made sense. Well it did, and it didn't. If the drawer was left open with me in it, nobody would have been able to pass between it and the table to get to the sink and the range. So presumably that meant they had to shut the drawer? I pondered on this for many years and was fully grown up before it dawned on me that they must have taken the drawer out of the chest and put it on their bed before laying their precious only daughter in it.

Precious or not, I was banished to sleep in the box room in the attic before too long. My brothers' room up there seemed a place of great joy to me. Each of their beds was placed under a section of slanted attic roof. On rare days when they wanted to make me laugh, they had a foolproof routine. I never tired of seeing them lie down, then bob up and hit their heads on the sloping ceilings. I hope my hysterical shrieks were compensation for their sore heads.

The box room where I slept was not a place of joy. Firstly, there was only a skylight, so it was never bright. Secondly, it stored a collection of old furniture which took on ghastly, ghostly shapes . Thirdly, it was cold. Fourthly, – and worst of all – I was alone. I could not see why I should have to sleep alone when my brothers had such japes together. And my parents had each other... in their nice cosy bed... in the kitchen. It became my routine to make a nightly trek to share that nice cosy bed, bumping down the steps of the curving stair, easing myself in through the kitchen door, climbing over my sleeping father, and settling into the warm groove next to my mother where I slept the contented sleep of the child who has got her way.

It wasn't long before my parents decided that getting my way was not good for me, or for them. I was told that I must NOT come down in the night and that if I did, I would be sent straight back up. The next few nights revealed the extent of their intent. I was shocked by their heartless disregard. Settling myself in the box room bed twice nightly doubled my pain, but I persisted with my nightly sorties, believing that their need for sleep would eventually force them to relent. Not so! Dire threats were issued, the nature of which I have expunged from my memory. There came a night when I was left in no doubt that not only was my presence   unwelcome,   but   there   would   be CONSEQUENCES if I dared to insinuate said presence into their time of rest.

I may have wiped the details of threatened punishment from my mind but I have not dispelled the demons from the night that followed – the shadowy shapes flitting among the sheet-covered furniture, the nasal, cracked voice at the door pleading 'Let me in, let me in'.

And there was more. When my fear and despair became all-consuming, I decided that I would *have* to go downstairs.

They would surely understand when I told them that someone had been calling at my door. I jumped out of bed onto the cold lino floor, ran the few steps across the room and put my hand out to turn the door handle. The handle wasn't there. The door wasn't there. A bare wall met my searching fingers. There was no way out.

Bewildered, I felt my way back to the cold, uninviting bed which awaited me that night and all the nights after. I remained bemused for years. Who had been calling to come in? How had my parents managed to move the door and replace it by morning? Most puzzling of all, why did they not welcome my nightly visits?

Coffee mornings

My father drank Camp coffee, a habit presumably adopted during the war. Children in the 1950s heard a lot about THE WAR. Despite its privations and terrors, so much good spirit was said to have existed during those years that there almost seemed some regret that the war was over.

My parents (and my older two brothers) saw out the war in London and had many a Blitz tale to tell. My then baby brother, Stephen, was left asleep in an Anderson shelter when everyone emerged after an attack, and was forgotten about for hours. My oldest brother, Paul, then around three years old, always heard the sinister Doodlebug bombs approaching before anyone else and would jump up and down in excitement, shouting, 'It's coming, it's coming!' Then came the silence while everyone waited to hear where the bomb had landed and, hopefully, to breathe again.

Aye, those of us born in the wake of the war were left in no doubt that we had missed Great Britain at its Greatest. That was when life had been lived to the full.

My father was an early riser and he enjoyed his cup of coffee at the start of the day. I'm not sure if I was an early riser by nature or whether my father liked a bit of his little girl's company without the boisterous bustle of the bothersome brothers, but when I was three, he would come up to my little room each morning and initiate our ritual of responses.

FATHER: Would you like a drink?
ME: Yes please, Daddy, can I have some coffee?
FATHER: Coffee?
ME: Yes, coffee. You know how I like it.
FATHER: How is it again?
ME: You know.
FATHER: I can't quite remember.
ME: You know. Just a little bit of coffee...
FATHER: Oh yes, a little bit of coffee and...
ME: ... and lots and lots and lots of sugar.

The war was over, but sugar rationing was not. I was jolly well going to get my share.

Back to front

After my father and I drank our coffee in the early morning, what else did we do? Well, there was the cat to feed, the cat who woke my father each day by jumping on the bed and licking his face. There was the breakfast table to set for the rest of the family and porridge to be stirred in the double saucepan.

But the main reason my father got up early was to read. Of course, he read at other times too. In fact he read at almost all times, including when crossing the road. Even before his behind touched the seat of the tram, underground train or bus he was travelling on, his left hand was feeling for the latest edition of *Trusting and Toiling** which would be stored in his inside pocket. It seemed he could listen to me prattle on and read at the same time. Well at least I thought he could...

While he read in the morning, so did I. No doubt, I looked at picture books at first, but I don't remember a time when I couldn't read. I *do* remember sitting on my father's knee, learning Hebrew words from a children's Hebrew picture book. What fun – we read it from back to front too!

---

* *Trusting and Toiling* was the magazine produced by the mission that my father worked for – *The Mildmay Mission to the Jews*.

*Me with my father on
the beach at Prestwick*

The chaos of family breakfast put an end to these studious pursuits as the boys were fed, scrubbed, brushed and packed off to school. No nursery for the 1950s preschool child, so I played outside in the back green or in the terrace at the front of the tenement. The terrace was accessed by steps from Newhall Street and was only the width of a pavement. Great for children playing out, but furniture removal firms must have dreaded a call to our street. All items had to be manhandled from Newhall Street to each close. There were four storeys of flats with attics above, and there were three flats on each level. Much Irn Bru must have been consumed by thirsty carriers.

The 'dyke' separated our street from the waste ground and railings on the banks of the River Clyde. Big children climbed over the dyke to play there but we littler ones were content to potter near the closes. Old Mrs Smith, who must have been one family's granny, sat outside and watched everything and talked to everyone. She could do magic with pieces of paper stuck to her fingers. 'Fly away Peter, fly away Paul,' she would say and the pieces of paper were gone. But then: 'Come back Peter, come back Paul,' and there they were again, stuck to the ends of her fluttering fingers. I was in daily awe.

Perhaps I was looking forward to watching this enthralling show on the morning that I managed to get more back to front than my Hebrew primer. I knew, as I worked my way down the four flights of stairs, that I really needed to go to the toilet. I'm afraid that, before I embarked on the long descent, I had told my mother I had already been. I thought that things would be alright, especially if I sat down at the top of the next flight. The trailing stream of liquid that snaked down the stairs said otherwise. So did my mother.

Getting into hot water

Of course we had heating in our house! We had a cosy range in the kitchen and that was where all life was lived. Heating in the bedrooms? Hardly! But we had some old fur coats someone had given my mother and it was quite snug when they were laid over the beds – at least, after a while.

Hot water? Well no, we didn't actually have a hot tap anywhere but there was hot water in the kettle on the range. What about the tap in the bathroom? You mean the toilet? Well, we didn't actually have a tap in the toilet. We washed our hands at the kitchen sink. What about the bath tap? Well, we didn't actually have a bath as such. Not one with taps. Just one of those zinc baths, that was carried into the kitchen on Saturday night and filled from the water heated on the range. Yes, it was a lot of work to fill it, which is why we took turns to bathe in the same water (in the dark kitchen with only the green light of the wireless to find the soap by). Guess who went in last? Well, I suppose it would have been too hot for me if I'd gone in first.

A meal fit for a queen?

The only sovereign that my family considered worth bothering about was the Sovereign Lord of Heaven and Earth. Worldly monarchs didn't carry much clout in our house. Still, Queen Elizabeth II was to be crowned on 2 June 1953 and while my parents' eyes may have been firmly fixed on the heavenly kingdom to come, we did still live in the earthly empire ruled by Great Britain.

Like most households in the land, we had a book of pictures of the young royal family. It seemed to me that the little Prince Charles and his sister, Princess Anne, were sweet children. I felt quite a connection with them as my birthday fell between theirs. I liked her blonde curls, I liked seeing him pedalling his little car but, as I had eczema, I *loved* the velvet collars on their winter coats.

Every tin of biscuits and toffees that year sported pictures of our young queen-to-be and her family. It was hard to avoid the excitement of it. Mrs Lorry, two closes along, had a television. We and other neighbours were invited to watch the Coronation there. (Even as I write that, I realise that her name must have been 'Laurie'. For over 60 years, I've been thinking what a funny name she had.) A new threat to discourage bad behaviour was instituted in our house: 'If you're not good, you won't be going to see the Coronation on television.' Sad to relate, Daniel and I were deemed 'not good' in some way and we were not to go to the great jamboree.

Now here's where the mists of time swirl a little uneasily. I don't remember seeing the Lorrys' television, let alone the Coronation being shown on it. Yet the rest of the family say that they were there watching it. Surely not even in the harsh old 1950s would two children, aged seven and three, have been abandoned at home during the Coronation? Yet I remember the guilt of the punishment being pronounced and the feeling of regret at being told I would not be going to see the momentous event.

On the other hand, I have a clear memory of sitting on the floor in the Lorrys' house eating a plate of baked beans while lots of people were milling about. Baked beans were my favourite food. I wouldn't be wrong about that.

The crowning insult

The new queen visited Glasgow not long after the coronation and the people turned out in masses to greet her. The crowds didn't line the pavements; they crammed the streets full to bursting, people ten deep in places. Not much chance for a three-year old to get a good view of our monarch, though lots of children were pushed through to the front to wave their little Union Jacks. Probably that explains how I saw her sitting in her golden coach drawn by black horses. I had a little metal model of it too. Yet the photographs insist that she was in a black sedan.

I know what I saw. I saw Queen Elizabeth ll waving from a golden coach with Prince Philip sitting beside her – but she wasn't wearing her crown and I was heartbroken.

She had the chance to get things right for me in 2012 when she came to Glasgow as part of her Jubilee Tour. My husband and I had an unexpected day off during the week. 'What on earth can we do on a rainy day in Glasgow? I said. 'I know, I'll Google *What to do in Glasgow*. Aha, let's go on a guided tour of the City Chambers. We've never done that before. It starts at 10.30am.'

'Good idea,' he said. So we drove into town and parked the car. 'The streets don't seem to have much traffic today' we observed, conversationally. 'Oh, and there are barriers blocking off George Street; oh, there are barriers right round George Square. Let's ask one of those officials what's going on.'

'The Queen is coming,' he said, clearly wondering what planet we'd alighted from.

This time it was accurate to say that the streets were *lined* with people. There was a single line of royal onlookers and lots of security people waiting to check the bags of the few.

'Let's rush round to the City Chambers. We've got one minute before the tour starts.'

The smiley lady at the desk said, 'Sorry, no tours today. We hardly ever cancel, but the Queen is coming.'

'Oh well, let's have a walk round the Cathedral instead.' I suggested, so we headed for the High Street.

Even from a distance, we could see flags waving.

'The Queen is coming,' the yellow-jacketed man told us. 'Oh, let's give in,' I said.' After all, it's 59 years since I last saw her. Surely twice in a lifetime is not too many times to see the Queen.' So we waited and we saw a little flash of pink in the car as she passed. She didn't have her crown on this time either. The difference was that this time I didn't cry.

Bursting the bubble

Paul (with Monty), me, Daniel, Stephen

My mother was the church organist and my father was a church deacon in Bridgeton Baptist Church. On a global scale, these offices may not rate highly, but in the nook of the world we inhabited, they commanded RESPECT. No doubt my father's calling as a missionary to Jews afforded us some special status in church circles too.

Not only that, but we kids were smart! Don't get me wrong; with our hand-me-down missionary children's clothes and an income to match, the best that could be said about our turn-out was – 'clean'. But, immodest as it may seem to say so, we were quick and clever with words, we read beyond our years, we were musical and we knew things, especially about the Bible. By the local standards of the day, we were smart. As the youngest of the family and the only girl, I was given much flattering attention by the local churchgoing women. In Sunday School, I might even have been considered a little prodigy.

So when our church planned a soirée with everyone doing their party piece, it was natural that some bright young Sunday School teacher should have the idea of teaching me a poem for the occasion. Even at four, I knew that this was my destiny. I was word-perfect for weeks and drove my brothers mad with constant performances of my piece. 'Stick your chin in,' they would snarl, 'nobody will see your face at all.' The word 'show-off' lay thick on the air.

My mentor was thrilled with my preparations and, on the night of the show, she brought me a little bar of soap in the shape of a dog. I was enchanted. Soap in our house came in chunky bars of Sunlight. The content of the poem eludes me, but the punchline was about making good use of soap. She gave me instructions that, as I said the final line, I should bring forth triumphantly, from behind my back, the said bar of soap.

My moment arrived and I mounted the stage. I stood with hands behind my back concealing the little bar of soap, and I faced the audience. The audience... the audience... an ocean of faces gazed up expectantly. I opened my mouth to speak but... the audience... the audience... They seemed so large and I was so little. I opened my mouth again... and again… and again, but no sound could I produce.

As instructed, I brought forth the bar of soap, it's import sadly lost without the relevant words, and then my moment was over. Strangely, it brought the house down.

I lathered away my confusion and disappointment with the little dog of soap.

Pollokshields, Glasgow

age 5–9

Sailing close to the wind

My brother Daniel was a boy of action. Standing still, sitting still, lying still was not for him. On one Fife holiday, I shared a bed with him. It was like being in bed with a litter of lively pups. Did he really have only the regular number of limbs? How did they get everywhere at once? My protests were heeded. I gratefully yielded my space to my long-suffering father and settled down beside the calmness of my mother.

My mother, me and Daniel

At home, my parents were expecting visitors from the Mission and preparations were being made to spruce things up for the guests. It was school holidays and things were a bit dull for Daniel, who was about eight at the time. He was full of enthusiasm for living – and full of bright ideas. He and I would go to the park, he decreed. We would go to Maxwell Park and we would sail our model boat.

Maxwell Park was two miles walk away. We were quite new to living in Pollokshields and we weren't too sure of the route. We were quite laden too. Daniel carried the boat and a long cane with which to guide its course. I carried a black straw-stuffed dog under one arm and a white straw-stuffed dog under the other.

Still, our journey was uneventful and before long – well, perhaps it was quite long – our boat was skimming across the water, white sails billowing. It was certainly not at all long before Daniel, cane in hand, leaned out over the water too far and fell right into the pond. Ever quick-witted, he somehow managed to turn himself over in the water and hold out the cane for me to grab to pull him out. Even though his face was under water, he seemed to be burbling instructions to me. Less quick-witted, shocked by the event, and hampered by the dogs I was holding, I couldn't work out how to grab the cane. Probably just as well; more than likely, I and my dogs would have joined him in the water. In the event, some older children got him out, though I have no idea how. I think I may have been having a little fit of the vapours at the time.

The other children raked through their pockets to see if they could pay for us to go home by bus. No one had enough money so we set out on the long walk home. This time I was detailed to carry the heavy boat as well as my two dogs. Daniel insisted that he would take the cane. 'It will give me strength,' he asserted.

Not too far from the park, a kind lady took pity on the dripping urchin and his fading sister. She took us to her house, dried Daniel off, fed us, phoned our home and soon our brother Stephen arrived to walk us home. We were mightily impressed with the lady's big Pollokshields mansion. We sat before a range in a huge kitchen whose sole function – as Stephen remarked in astonishment – was as a place in which to prepare food!

We were in no hurry to go home. And indeed, our reception there was decidedly mixed. But Daniel would always claim that there had been an unforeseen bonus to our adventure: 'I swam a stroke that day,' he would declare proudly.

Christmas wonder

The contents of a Christmas stocking in the 1950s were mostly predictable. The tangerine wrapped in coloured tissue filled the toe; pencils, rubber and ruler measured the length; and balloons, one or two *Made in Hong Kong* toys, some sweets and nuts would be scattered throughout. Sometimes writing paper upon which to write the after-Christmas thank you letters appeared. Did tangerines smell more pungently then or we were just less accustomed to the aroma? Your nose would tell you when Santa had made his annual visit; that, and the pleasantest possible weight over your legs as you lay in bed.

Larger (though not very large) presents would be under the Christmas tree and we were in no doubt as to who had given us what. Santa did not deal in Meccano, paints, dolls or books. These came from our parents, our aunts, or family friends. Sometimes, welcome gifts of money promised a post-Christmas shopping expedition to town. The whole season was every bit as gut-churningly thrilling then as the whole excess-laden bonanza seems to be for children now.

Mr Fernie kept the local newsagent's shop. For a few weeks before Christmas, his shop window blazed with toys. One side of the double-fronted shop was devoted to sweets, cigarettes, pipe tobacco, matches, shoelaces, soap, clay for washing tenement stairs, and... even a few newspapers. The other side of the shop, including a display window, was given over to the trappings of children's pastimes and amusements The window didn't change much during the year, except for the marble season, the ball season, the scrap season, the stamp season, the skipping season... But in December, Mr Fernie excelled himself; our palates were daily teased with new and ever more desirable toys.

It was two days before Christmas when I saw the teddy. He sat, golden and furred, with a red, satin ribbon around his sweet neck. He wasn't large – perhaps a foot long – just the perfect size for a six-year old to cuddle and caress. And he was put there for me. I had never been more certain of anything. Already I could feel his soft firmness; already I had named him Rupert.

I rushed home to tell my parents – not that I wanted this bear. No, no, I actually NEEDED this bear. I absolutely HAD TO HAVE this bear for Christmas. They looked at me in consternation, and perhaps a little pity. The bear cost 17 shillings and sixpence. It was two days before Christmas. They had done their festive shopping and there was not a spare sixpence around. It was a fraught time as I wrestled with a love which was not to blossom. Only so much of a relationship can be conducted standing in the street looking through the glass of a shop window. I went to bed on Christmas Eve in a fervour of anticipation. My head told me, as my parents had, that the bear could not be mine but my heart said something else.

It always seemed to me that my parents spent the night before Christmas walking back and forth from their bedroom to the kitchen, rustling paper as they went. From my bedroom in between these two rooms, I could chart each journey but could never work out what on earth they could be doing. Our gift pile was never so lavish next morning that it could have justified that amount of bustle and yet it happened every year. It was my brothers' habit to spend much of December trying to unearth any presents that might have been concealed around the house; perhaps my parents spent much of Christmas Eve trying to remember those hiding places. They could have saved themselves the bother. The boys could have told them.

When I woke, it was dark and quiet and I knew it must be very early morning. The longed-for weight of my filled stocking pinned my legs to the bed. We were under strict instructions not to open our stockings until morning proper when my parents were up. I certainly wouldn't have dared put the light on. But they hadn't said anything about not feeling my stocking had they? I felt its length, its weight, its knobbles, I heard the crackly sound of something wrapped in cellophane. I moved the stocking around the better to relish the sensations. What sounded like gunshots spattered the dark silence and I lay back, guilty and frightened. As my heart resumed its normal speed, I realised that the sound had been made by the hard-shelled nuts falling out of my stocking and bouncing one by one on my lino-ed floor.

It took some time before I could summon the nerve to return to the stocking inspection. The cellophane-wrapped package was stuck in at the top. It was too bulky to fit into the stocking. It didn't conform to any of the expected shapes of gift. Better not pull it out, though, in case more nut avalanches were started.

I lay down again and speculated. I sat up again. My little, wondering hands kneaded the hardnesses below the crackling paper. I thought perhaps I could feel a small, firm nose. Could these hard roundnesses be the wonderful, rich brown eyes that had stared into mine through the glass of the shop window? Without pulling the parcel out from its place in the stocking, I took hold of the middle of it and squeezed. A deep-throated bear roar ripped forth. Even if they hadn't heard the nuts falling, they would surely hear that.

I lay down again. I was content.

Happily ever after

I was going to be eight! I was going to have a party! My parents must have been worn down by my nagging. I never remember any of my brothers having a birthday party. Never mind! Invitations had been distributed! My birthday was two days after Christmas, and the party was arranged for a day during the school holidays. I was feverish with excitement!

Or perhaps just feverish? An expert hand on my heated brow pronounced me to be ill. And so I was. Measles had struck me down on the eve of my favourite time of year: Christmas, my birthday and, this once, my party. Measles with the rash, the cough, the fever, the darkened room, the boredom. I was low, very low.

I was lifted a little by a gift from Miss Black, a kind, gentle family friend. It was a pink brush and comb set for my long hair. I was cheered.

I opened my Christmas gift from Auntie Rachel. It was a brown brush and comb set. My good cheer was a little dimmed.

I always looked forward to opening my birthday present from my Auntie Janet. She always did me proud, and this year the package was big. It was a large display box. In it nestled a blue brush and comb set. It was getting harder to keep my spirits up.

It was decided that the party would have to be postponed till measles was conquered. Paul was sent round to the guests' houses to break the news. He returned with gifts intended to be given at my party. There were red hair ribbons, blue hair ribbons, and... a hair brush. I was low, very low. I felt defined by my hair.

It was some comfort to know that my friend, Margaret, who lived across the road also languished in bed with measles. Her father visited me and brought over a present – a copy of *Hans Andersen's Fairy Tales*. I was not allowed to read for fear of damage to my eyes but my father sat by my bed and transported me to the land of *The Snow Queen, The Red Shoes, The Ugly Duckling...*

Who needed parties?

The life and soul. . .

Actually my party did take place when measles was behind me and many of my friends. Having talked my not-very-party-minded parents into hosting this event, I then realised our home, our purse and my parents were ill-equipped to deliver what was expected. I'd been to parties. The tables sparkled with cold meat sandwiches made with white bread, and lashings of 'ginger' (fizzy drinks). Ginger was never going to happen. No, my mother decreed. We could have Creamola Foam to drink. And there would be healthy, brown bread sandwiches filled with mashed banana; a little jam would add extra sweetness. I was distraught but she held firm.

My father had a bright idea. The mission owned a projector. It didn't show movies, but film-strips, which were rows of coloured transparencies joined together in a roll. A written narrative was read out as the pictures were changed. My father would send for a children's film strip and show it at the party. My heart leapt. No-one else would have a projector. Of course, continued my father, it would be a Christian film-strip so it would be an opportunity to witness as well. My heart plummeted. I saw my social rating shifting from exotic to downright peculiar.

We sat down at the table and faced the dull-looking brown sandwiches. Amongst the skills my mother had acquired during her nursing years was the ability to cut bread in paper-thin slices. The sandwiches were moist and sweet. Before many minutes she was running to the kitchen to produce more of the same – and again, more of the same. Was that a little giggle of triumph that I heard bubbling up as she placed another plate before our eager eyes, hands and mouths?

The Creamola Foam seemed to go down unexpectedly well too. As well as drinking the sweet froth, endless fun could be had spooning the powder into a cup, filling it with water, stirring it up, and watching the white spume flood up and over. Or you could lick the dry powder and get a mind-blowing fizzy buzz. I was pleasantly surprised at the mood of the partygoers.

My father announced the filmstrip. Expectations were high and the audience a little restive for the show to start. My father was a scholar. Technical matters were not his gift. He wore a pocket watch on an albert chain, for goodness sake, because he couldn't get a wristwatch to work on him! If there was a wrong way to fit the film holder, he found it. The pictures were upside down and sideways; more than once the whole strip was shown from the finish to the start. As his frustration mounted and even spilled over into an exasperated 'ehh' or three, the hysteria of the gaggle of eight-year olds soared.

Nobody wanted the film strip to work properly. No picture story could have created so much merriment. The whole fiasco was recalled with shrieking giggles for months after. Hmmm... my father an (albeit unconscious) comic?

The final triumph was a thespian *tour de force* on the part of my mother. One of my chums was led blindfold over an obstacle course which she'd been shown beforehand. The great joke, of course, was that all the obstacles had been removed, and my mother, with many graphic injunctions, was making the child step over and around the empty space with ridiculously exaggerated gestures. My guests were weeping with laughter.

Simple pleasures indeed. Perhaps it was time to review my perception of my parents?

My parents and me in our back green

Like it or lump it

My father collected books insofar as his slender means ever exceeded the needs of his growing family. Despite my mother being the actual human embodiment of a Household Encyclopedia, he had at some time invested in four huge volumes which were the last word on cooking, laundry, DIY, how things worked and a myriad other topics related to running a home. Perhaps he bought the books before he was married. He was, after all, 46 years old before he took the marital plunge. Some practical know-how might have come in handy before that, although I saw little evidence of his having benefitted from the possession of those weighty tomes.

But they were fun for us to look at, especially the volumes which sported shiny coloured pictures of rich and gaudy desserts. I have read of starving people fantasising about food. Well, we were not starving but, despite my mother's ingenuity, our fare was plain and limited. I cannot now recapture the satisfaction which Daniel and I derived from our perusal of these pages. We would take turns to choose a confection and then go through the motions of eating it. The activity always ended in the same way: unseemly grabbing at every dish on the page, when polite turn-taking ceased to thrill the palate.

Real-life eating led to the most regular and keenly fought battles between me and my mother. My mother was brought up in a orphanage. She described some the daily fare she received there .There was bread dipped in cocoa, bread dipped in dripping, and for a treat, bread dipped in treacle. I suppose it was understandable that she should have scant tolerance for my dainty appetite but my sensitive tastebuds were very real to me.

Shall I list my dislikes? Quicker to list my likes. Nothing topped Baked Beans. It was my custom to scrape clean both the bean tin and the bean saucepan to relish every last drop of the sweet tomato sauce which enveloped the soft, chewy nuggets. I was quite partial to triangles of Dairylea cheese, as much for the ritual of unwrapping the silver paper as for savouring the dense texture and creamy taste. Marmite was a family favourite but I rather favoured my bread spread with salad cream.

I ate most of the rest of what I was served reluctantly and slowly. My brothers ate everything voraciously and quickly. They watched my slow deliberations at teatime in particular. There was sometimes a slice of fruit cake for each of us. Though I didn't like it, it was a valuable bargaining tool; sometimes it seemed worth working my way through just for the unaccustomed sense of power. 'You're just eating that for the sake of it,' they would say in scorn and disappointment. It was true, but I would have gone to my death defending my right to plod through the dry, currant-ridden slab.

When it came to things made with milk, the battleground was bloody. My tears and screams were poor weapons beside my mother's determination to properly nourish her child. In vain did my brothers try to humour me by turning on switches to activate my internal eating machine. I was charmed by the novelty, but the lumps of rice pudding, tapioca and sago could not be smoothed out by any of their ploys. Though I knew I would yet again be banished to my cold room for the evening, I would not surrender.

I was invited to go on holiday with friends of the family. On the first day of my stay, rice pudding was served. I could not bring myself to refuse the proffered bowl in this house of kindness and generosity. With barely controlled retching, I swallowed down the creamy globules.

'Well done,' my hostess patted my shoulder, 'your mother did mention you didn't like rice pudding.'

The battle was lost.

A trip to the far east

Holidays! It didn't really matter how far you went, did it? It was all about a change of scene. Prestwick, Alva, Stirling were all fine places to go. One year, we went all the way to Selkirk. That was fully 80 miles! We took a hut in the country for two weeks. All household linen and clothes for six had to be taken with us. A big brown trunk was sent on ahead and we carried smaller cases on the bus. At the last minute, six of us became seven. Our parents, ever mindful of their Christian duty, decided to take with us James, a boy from the next close who had a 'bad family' and 'needed a holiday'.

Perhaps my parents should have been alerted by the word *hut* rather than *cottage* or *cabin* in the advert. Perhaps it would have made no difference if the price, which I certainly hope reflected the facilities, was right. Facilities? Well, to be fair, there were actually *two* huts. One for sleeping in and one for cooking in. 'Sensible,' you say 'keeping the stove away from the sleeping quarters.' Stove? Wouldn't you need electricity for that? We cooked on an open fire. Much of our holiday was spent walking to, from, and in the woods, gathering fuel for the greedy flames which cooked our tea. Tea! Ah yes – tea needs water. In fact, lots of things need water: cooking, washing, dishes, toilets.

(L to R) Stephen, Paul, Daniel, James.
Without their partings and slicked down hair,
my brothers look quite different – almost contemporary!

When we weren't gathering wood, we were bearing picturesque china pitchers to and from the not-so-nearby farmhouse to quench our water needs. Don't ask about the toilet. I have been unable to recover any memory of that. I guess that says it all.

I slept on a lumpy 'bed-chair' while my brothers were two to each small bed. Not sure who shared with James; our family may have been a bit scruffy but – my mother was a nurse, for goodness sake – we were *clean*.

For ever after, my mother was known to hold forth on the beauties of Selkirk and the wonderful holiday we had there.

James collecting water in a china pitcher

Al fresco dishwashing
Is my father assessing the size of the task before him while he waits for the basin of hot water to be brought? Or is he thinking of the book he could be reading if he were at home?

Catcall

We always had a cat. We usually had a cat called Monty – named, with commendable patriotism, after Field Marshall Montgomery. We had four cats in succession with that name. It seems strange that four imaginative, well-read children couldn't think of a new name for each new moggy. My father, who enjoyed a bit of word-play, had other names for our cat – some of which he made into a little ditty sung to the tune of *I will make you fishers of men*. It went:

> *China, china,*
> *china our 'erb*
> *Are you superb*
> *Or only suburb?*

Today's cats must be a cannier breed to survive in our traffic-laden streets. Our cats all lost their lives on the not-very-busy roads near our house. Such was the grieving that my brothers donned black armbands and our mother would declare through tears that we were never, ever getting another cat. Somehow we always did. Perhaps we didn't change the name in the hope that our mother would forget that we'd had to get a replacement cat.

Daniel and beloved cat. This one was not called Monty.
In a flight of creativity, he was named Ginger.

Our cats were usually male and were always 'dressed'. It was never spelled out quite what this entailed, but we were told that it was a good thing to do as it encouraged them to stay at home. The process was certainly not painless (no anaesthetic for male cats at that time) but it was quick and relatively cheap. Somehow a female kitten came to join our family. Perhaps 'Monty' was not such a suitable name for her? Discussion took place. No decision was reached.

It was decreed that the little lady also should be dressed – to stop her having kittens. What this had to do with dressed males not leaving home I was not sure, but the decision was taken and enquiries were made. My mother was horrified to find that the operation would cost 25 shillings. We were horrified to find that the kitten would have to stay at the vet's overnight to recover from the anaesthetic. On the appointed day, we said au revoir to the little ball of fluff and mischief who was unaware of the ordeal before her. My father, who was the champion of all our cats, took her round to the vet. He was gone a long time. Far longer than it should take to hand over one small feline.

Finally he returned. We rushed to hear his report. He put his hand inside the top of his overcoat and plonked our cowering kitten down on the table.

'10/6,'* he said roughly, 'it's a tom.'

Monty it was then.

---

* 10/6: ten shillings and sixpence, less than half of the cost of the operation for a female cat.

In The Heat Of The Night

Bed, when first breached, could be a mighty cold place. I would arrive in my unheated bedroom, still swathed in the heat of the kitchen – a bit like Charlie Brown's friend, Pig-Pen, who always appeared enveloped in a cloud of dirt. But by the time I got into bed, I had shed most of that haze of warmth along with my clothes.

The best, though sadly forbidden, means to shake off the shivers produced by the chill of the sheets was to entice the cat to sneak in beside me. I would lift up the covers, pat the bed vigorously and make encouraging clicking noises until the cat deigned to comply. Not that he would ever admit that he wanted to; he made it clear that he just could not endure any more of my demeaning pantomime.

Oh, the luxury of snuggling up against that warm, furry body which took on the contours of mine and lay beside me, purring contentment. Oh, the shock of my cosy cocoon being shattered when the blankets were whipped back by an irate mother who had just noticed the cat's absence from the kitchen and put two and two together.

It was worth the scolding to wallow for a while in that velvet warmth – especially when the alternative was… The Hot Water Bottle.

Today's hot water bottles, though still not a patch on a cat, have soft fleecy covers and can be moulded to the shape of the user. The hot water bottle of my childhood was an unyielding aluminium cylindrical flask. With apologies to the *little girl with the curl* of nursery rhyme fame, when that bottle was hot, it was very very hot, and when it was cold, it was horrid.

If one chilly little toe so much as made fleeting contact with the bottle's scalding surface, the first sensation was of touching ice – before the blistering hotness seared its message into the brain. Sometimes the vessel slipped from the bed in the still of the night, falling to the uncarpeted floor with a terrifying clatter, and banging around noisily while the water glopped and slopped within its metal prison. Despite the noise, it was a relief when the bottle was gone. If it remained, I could instantly be jolted into full wakefulness in the early morning when that same little toe, now comfortable and snug, inadvertently brushed against the solid lump of ice-cold metal which blemished the end of my bed.

When I told my family that I had been writing down the stories of my childhood with which they were so conversant, right away some of them said, 'Is there one about the hot water bottle?'

Well, there wasn't… not the most inspiring topic after all… but… ach, they did so love to hear about it… so… here it is.

What's in a name?

Nobody else that I knew was called *Esther*. Some children hadn't even heard the name before. You always knew those who were familiar with The Bible because they were the only ones who knew to spell my name with an 'h'.

Nobody else had parents called *Olive* and *Eli*. When we played the 'footsteps game' where you had to take a step forward if you had an Uncle Jimmy or an Auntie Margaret, I was often left at the starting line until a friend took pity on me and called out: 'Take a step forward if you've got an Uncle Nathan or a cousin Blanche'.

I dreaded having to tell people my name. 'Oh that's lovely, and so unusual,' they'd simper. I'd squirm, and long to be able to say 'Alison' or 'Irene'.

When people come to choose names for a new baby, some names are ruled out because of the memory of someone who defined that name's character for them. Looking round my far-off primary classroom, I see Marjorie, with a huge bow holding her hair back, and a rather unreliable bladder; rosy-cheeked Iris, with a tiny voice which drove teachers mad; ringletted Carol, so sweet that, even when she was sick on the desk, she produced a delicate pink and white pile; and languid Lorna, who lived next door to the school but was always late.

I'm tortured by the sight of Alan, blonde and dozey; when the bell our teacher tied round his wrist didn't do the trick, she would push him up and down the classroom aisle to waken him up. There was naughty James, who got the belt within the first few days of Primary One. There was good-looking James, whom I arranged to meet in a close on my way home from the library. (We planned to kiss, but were too scared.) There was studious Isaac, who looked just as his name suggested; and there was clever Charles, golden of skin and of prospects.

Then there was Christopher, freckled, dark haired, rosy cheeked, with twinkly eyes and an infectious grin. I liked the boy but I *loved* his name which was a bit unusual in our circles. I promised myself it would be the name for my first son. Which it was.

When I remarried, my new husband showed me some pictures of himself as a boy. Guess what? It was just like looking at Christopher. The smile, freckles, big teeth and shock of dark hair were all right there.

Playing ball

My friends were always talking about going to have tea at their auntie's, or playing with their big cousins, or staying overnight with their grandparents. We had no living grandparents and we had no relatives at all in Scotland. Though we didn't see much of our relatives, my parents did keep in touch with their siblings by letter and we knew plenty about their lives. How flimsy seemed the paper of the thrice-folded airmail letters from my mother's sister, Auntie Jessie, in South Africa. Yet these frail-looking missives had crossed continents. It was thrilling to glean her news from the spidery writing which adorned every area of the blue surface, often making a border round the main text so that the letter had to be turned round and round to read every last word.

I felt important to be able to tell my friends that I was going to visit my aunts, Rose and Rachel, in England. Auntie Rose was one of my father's older sisters and Auntie Rachel, one of his younger. Neither had married and they lived together for many years in Hove, Sussex. There were seven children in my father's family. Although Lazarus died during WWI, he and five of the other siblings converted from Judaism to Christianity at different times in their lives.

For some years Rachel and Rose were members of the Exclusive Brethren who, as their name suggests, kept themselves apart from anyone who was not a membe of the sect. There was sparse contact between them and us during that period. Much to my father's joy, they emerged into the Open Brethren – still strict, but willing to engage once more with family. After all, *blood is thicker...*

My father's sister, Auntie Rachel.
A good Brethren woman always wore her hat.

Rose and Rachel must have been in their mid-sixties, and I around six, when my mother and I visited them. Both sisters were small and dumpy, had strong Lancashire accents, and spoke straight from the shoulder. They were not used to entertaining small children but thought they could manage a trip to the park with me. We stood in a triangle, tossing a ball between us. I got excited pretty quickly. When my aunt dropped the ball, I shouted 'Pick it up! Pick it up quick!"

'Pick it up, *please*,' said Auntie Rose.

Would I say it?

'Pick it up, *please*,' repeated Auntie Rachel.

Really, what would it have cost me? But I could not, would not, let those six placatory letters out of my mouth.

'If you can't say *please*, then we can't play ball. We'll just have to go home.' Auntie Rose's voice was monotonous and dogged.

I'd heard these kind of threats from adults before. 'If you don't... then you can't...' Sometimes they didn't come to anything if you stood your ground.

I stood my ground.

Auntie Rose stood her ground.

We returned home, my spirits more deflated than the ball.

Aye, blood is thicker...

Amen to that

Wednesday night was Prayer Meeting night at the church. For three hours, the Cohen children were at home on their own!

The evening often started with a rousing game of 'Balloony Ball'. In teams of two, we defended and attacked the 'goals' at either end of our hall with a balloon which we battered back and forth, and which we must keep off the floor at all costs. It was not a game which could be played quietly. My brothers were by this point galumphing teenagers. Sometimes more than the balloon was battered. The game was usually ended prematurely by command of our long-suffering downstairs neighbour.

If there were biscuits in the house at the start of the evening, there weren't by the end. If anyone had any money, I could be bribed to run across to Albert's café to choose some 'dees'* and we would wallow in an orgy of sweets.

Best of all was when Paul tuned our wireless away from the usual, worthy Home Service or more highbrow Third

---

* 'Dees' from 1d, or one penny – my brothers' name for the items on the 'penny tray'. Of course, all sweets on the tray were unwrapped and you could pick out the ones you wanted with your own fair fingers!

Programme to wicked, decadent, depraved Radio Luxembourg. Then we could catch up and sing along with the current Top Twenty. Oh, we were thankful indeed for that Prayer Meeting! Without it we would have been sadly out of touch with popular culture.

Of course, homework must be finished by 9.15pm when our parents were due home. There might just have been one or two spats before that. Daniel was rather prone to nosebleeds when punched. Often some energetic mopping up of his clothes and face was needed before we could generate the calm atmosphere of study which my parents would expect to find on their return.

New for old

My mother could make new clothes out of old. She did it all the time. She cut down worn men's suits to make trousers for my brothers. She ripped out wool from misshapen garments and used it to knit pullovers. She made me dresses out of skirts and skirts out of dresses. Even in her eighties, she would crochet a new collar onto an old top and give it a fresh look.

We were less enthusiastic about the products of her skills than she was over plying them. She spent many hours cutting down an adult coat to create one for the seven-year-old me. I did wear it once, but despite my guilt over my mother's wasted labour, I could not face it again. Well, it was a fur coat! No little girls that I knew wore fur coats. Ah, mother dear, you were way ahead of your time.

When a garment could no longer be fashioned into another, it moved into the next phase of its useful life. It became part of a bedmat. A bedmat had soft material on one side, old blanket in the middle, and squares from discarded garments stitched together in a patchwork on top. All our beds sported these warm, heavy, historical documents. Generations of clothes and their wearers could be identified in them and a host of memories revived at the sight.

'There's that dress that Auntie Janet wore to our wedding. Oh, that's a bit of that lovely costume I had made for me when I was nursing. Of course that's before I knew your father. In those days I could afford to get things made for me. Now I have to be the tailor for everybody.'

When it was sewing season, we ate off half of the kitchen table. The rest of the table was given over to our splendid Singer sewing machine. I loved the look of this grand old lady, I loved the sound of it, the smell of it, the ritual of threading it. I loved the smooth rolling action, the well-turned metal. I loved to see it being carefully oiled. I loved to slide open the wooden lid at one end and reveal the cosy nest in which were squirrelled away cotton reels, bobbins, snap fasteners, elastic, and the mysteriously named *petersham*. I loved the huge sturdy case it was stored in and I loved to turn the handle as my mother guided the material.

My mother treasured her sewing machine but, as we were not always around to turn the handle, she longed for it to be motorised. Then she would always have two hands free to keep the stitching straight. Besides, turning the handle was jolly hard work. By the time her dream was realised and the machine was powered, my brothers were of an age to buy their own trousers. But my wardrobe continued to flourish, and my mother delighted in the ease of using the pedal instead of the power of her arm.

Eventually, the machine became mine. It was old, it was heavy, it was bulky. I swapped it for a new, light, modern model.

I've had four now.

A sack of gold

Collecting empty lemonade bottles and returning them to shops to claim the threepence deposit was a popular way for children to augment their pocket money. It was frowned on by my mother: 'You never know where those bottles have been'. I won't say that we never did it, but if we did, it was a clandestine pursuit.

But there was one occasional little earner which was sanctioned by my mother. As a missionary family, we were given gifts of second-hand clothing. Parcels sometimes arrived – even from America! – full of unusual clothes which other people thought might be useful to us. Well, on occasion they were, and my mother was grateful.

It was fun to try on odd-looking garments at home. It was not so much fun to have to wear them in public and face the comments of my less fortunate friends, whose wardrobes were not endowed with such exotic creations, and whose parents were obliged to buy their clothes in shops.

Even allowing for my mother's ingenuity with a needle, there were some items which were never going to be worn again by anyone, anywhere, ever. These were consigned to one or other of my mother's two ragbags. We watched these bags with interest – 'vested interest' you might say. When my mother declared that the bags were full, there would be an unaccustomed clamour of volunteers to carry them the half mile to their next destination.

J.Rodgers, Rag Merchant conducted business in a wooden shack opposite Shields Road underground station. Lit by a single, bare lightbulb, its murky shadow-filled depths hinted at nefarious deeds. The huge bulging sacks which lined the walls might well have been filled with body parts.

J.Rodgers herself, as we thought she was, materialised from the gloom to take our bags with her fingerless-gloved hands. Red, and rather grimy faced, she was never seen without a felt hat topping her grey straggle of hair. Bundled up in layers of cardigans, coats and shawls, she looked to be mutating into the goods she dealt in.

In the centre of the hut hung THE SCALES. She would humph our now pitiably-small-seeming offerings onto the flat wooden platform on one side of this contraption. We watched her plonk the metal weights onto the counter-balance tray, aware that our future spending power depended on her conclusions. She would mutter her calculations, then stomp off to the little partitioned-off counting house. She extracted a few coins from her money box and grudgingly placed them in our eager hands. The whole operation was carried out without eye contact or conversation.

Well, nearly. I did say that my mother had two ragbags. One was filled with any kinds of fabric, but the other was the Sack of Gold. It held items made from wool only; the price given for these was much much higher than for other materials. Always a smaller bag than the other, we would place it in the hands of Judge Rodgers with great care, and some trepidation. It was opened and inspected as a suspicious package at airport security might be in the present day. Woollen items were put together to be weighed. Anything which did not pass her stringent wool test was thrown to the side with a sniff and a single comment. Her words became an oft-repeated mantra for us and never failed to provoke rueful mirth. On each visit to her lair, we waited, with barely suppressed giggles, for this one moment of verbal communication.

The words were spat at us with a hoarse, contemptuous snarl.

'That's no wool, sonny.'

On first-name terms

My tonsils were a pain in the neck! Though I enjoyed the odd day off school, I wasn't so keen on the sore throat, the fever and the prescribed treatment – gargling four times a day with a purple liquid made from dissolved crystals of permanganate of potash. Aside from the foul taste, I was mystified by my parent's injunction, 'Be careful not to swallow any. It's very poisonous, you know.' There seemed to be a mixed message being given out here. Either they wanted to cure me or they didn't.

In common with most of my peers, the problem was solved at a cut – by the removal of the offensive organs. I won't dwell on the few days in hospital. Suffice to say that the promised ice cream (with which I was lured to agree to the whole procedure in the first place) only appeared on the final day just as my father came to take me home. I didn't stay to eat it. On the bright side, I did find a very exciting war story in the ward library and was shaken to my very innards when I read about thumb screws being applied to a young girl in the Resistance. It gave me a brief respite from my own perceived torture.

Before the great excision, I could count on frequent days off school with burning throat and head. 'Off school' meant 'in bed'. 'In bed' meant that people brought you food, drinks and hot water bottles from the kitchen. My mother's wafer-thin slices of bread and marmite were often all I could summon the strength to face.

But sometimes the service could be a bit slow. Since my room was next to the kitchen, I could never understand why they couldn't hear my calls. It didn't occur to me that they might be doing something other than awaiting my pleasure.

'Mummy! Mummy! Daddy!'

I became desperate for the sight of a friendly face, for bread, for tea, for a word, for a sign that I was not forgotten so soon. Despairing, I unleashed my secret weapon.

'Olive! Olive! Eli!'

It worked – though the faces were not friendly.

Bricks, buttons and bibles

I t was a cold, wet Sunday evening and, in keeping with the elements, both Daniel and I were a bit under the weather. It was decided that we should be allowed to stay at home and miss the evening service. We didn't demur.

An evening off church! No prayers, no readings, no hymns, no sermon! How best should we use this gift of time? Let's build something with our bricks? Hmmm. Somewhat beneath the sophistication of the eleven-year old Daniel. My mother had an old toffee tin rattling with buttons of every size and colour, harvested from discarded garments. How about playing with the buttons? Hardly...

Undeterred, I began to build on the kitchen table. Daniel couldn't resist watching, and then commenting, and then putting a brick or two in place himself. 'I know,' I said, hopefully, 'Let's build a church.'

It was a moment of divine inspiration. We set to, and there on the table appeared the inside of our church, complete with pews, pulpit, even a rickety gallery. I fetched the button tin, and we walked families of buttons up the aisles and sat them on the pews, big ones carrying littler ones as coins for 'the collection'.

Whose idea was it to hold an actual service? I can't say,

but it wasn't me who read the bible text, it wasn't me who said the prayers and it wasn't me who preached the sermon convicting the buttons of their sins.

It wasn't exactly an evening off church.

Like billyoh

Ach, I wished I could join the Boys' Brigade! Fridays after school were given over to preparation for my brothers' weekly inspection at the BB. Polishing was my pleasure and that was lucky for the boys. Shoes, belts, buckles, badges and the brass button on the white haversack all had to gleam like billyoh, as my father would say.

Oh, the importance I felt as I put polish on the shoes with one brush, rubbed it off with another and did the final buffing with a corduroy pad. The belt buckle which bore the BB insignia was tricky to clean as dirt got in the grooves but an old toothbrush could help. I was seldom trusted with the job of applying blanco with a paintbrush to the white lines on their pill-box hats, though I was sure I could do it better than they did.

Hair brushed and greased down, the regalia must be donned perfectly, belt not covering any bit of the 'sack' of the haversack, belt buckle right in the centre of the front of the jacket and two tucks in the back of the jacket to make it lie smoothly.

Ach, the whole paraphernalia was wasted on boys!

Once a year, at the BB display, we got to see what went on at their weekly meetings. What an evening of delights! I was fascinated by the formation marching, I admired the boys' smart salutes, I clapped like billyoh as they received awards, I waited breathlessly for the announcement of the winner of 'The BB Boy of the Year' award.

Best of all was the PE display and the best bit of the that was the vaulting. My heart beat like billyoh as the feats became ever more daring. When the wooden springboard was put in place, the noise of sixteen-year old lads leaping from it over a wooden horse was thunderous. But they didn't just jump over the *horse*. Ever more boys, with heads tucked down, sat on the mat on the far side of the horse and the bigger boys jumped clear over *them* too.

Oh but I've forgotten the human pyramid! That really was The Best! They stood on each other's shoulders in a line, four boys high, with the smallest boy climbing the mountain of vest-clad bodies to teeter on the summit. Swaying and wobbling, could they hold the pose through the applause? Down they would tumble in a laughing, writhing heap of flailing limbs.

Ach, I wished I could join the Boys' Brigade!

Transfer of power

Living in a mission house entailed certain duties, not all of them unpleasant. One was to put up men from mission headquarters who had 'come up from London'. They came to speak at churches and mission halls about the work of my father's mission, The *Mildmay Mission to the Jews*. Men with exotic sounding eastern-European names like Krolenbaum or Loblinsky were regular guests in our home. Though it meant I had to give up my bedroom for a few days, the improvement in food during their stay was fair compensation.

The *Hebrew Christian Alliance* met in our house on the last Friday of the month. The sitting room would be filled with people whose names confirmed their connection to the Diaspora. These Jewish Christians, and others who 'loved the Jewish people', met in our house for a time of worship and prayer. Ever the show-off, I delighted in opening the door to each arrival, receiving their compliments, interest and, occasionally, their gifts. In return, I helped with the preparations. I unstacked and set out the chairs with a hymn book on each, I laid out the thick white cups and saucers, milk, sugar and Marie biscuits on the hall sideboard, and I helped to hand them round in the 'time of fellowship' after the meeting.

Dressed in Sunday best. Paul is holding Monty. Our visitor, Mr Krolenbaum, is benignly overseeing us. I am ensuring that the lining of my coat is visible. That was the only bit of the coat I liked.

Friday night was Boys' Brigade night for my brothers, so they were not usually around for this high society mingling. But there was one Friday when Stephen was at home. Ever curious on scientific matters, it seemed to him to be an interesting experiment to touch the two points of a pair of scissors to two electrical wires in our wireless. I believe it was during the prayer session in the sitting room that the power was lost. That coincided with the flash of excess power in the kitchen. Pale and shaken, my brother survived.

Whole food

When I think of Mr Boyd, I think of 'glow' and the letter 'v'. The glow came from within him and shone out of his light blue eyes. It was the glow of purity. He seemed untainted by our bad old world – and it showed. Despite those soft eyes being fixed on the glories of the next life, Mr Boyd treated his body like the holy temple he believed that it was. The letter 'v' related to the fact that he was vegetarian, anti-vivisection and anti- vaccination.

As the photograph suggests, Miss Altham and Mr Boyd

were not a couple. He rented a room in her four-in-a-block home in Croftfoot and she looked after him. He was not wordly enough to have the money or the savvy to run his own home. Miss Altham spoke slowly and loudly in her strong Lancashire accent, the little box of her hearing aid emitting squeaks and whistles which hinted at a limited usefulness. She cared for her charge with tenderness and loyalty. She seemed to sense that he was a rare flower to be cherished.

In his little room in her home were tinctures, pills and potions derived from natural sources. His smooth skin, ruddy cheeks and calm brow would have been an advertiser's delight.

I liked it when he came to visit us. He took me on his knee, he talked to me, he listened to me. He had time. Sometimes he ate with us and my father would ask him to bless the food. Eyes closed, head raised, he would sing in a sweet, light, quavering voice, his face transformed by adoration for his Maker.

> *What shall we render, our heavenly friend to thee,*
> *For care so tender for love so free?*

The tune was that of a German drinking song. The words were his own. There were three verses, each eight lines long. As I said, he had time. Best not to serve the food until he'd finished.

Who wears the pants?

My interest in my appearance was variously shaped and largely curtailed by my father and his ally, the Bible. Both Exodus and Deuteronomy stated that pierced ears are a mark of slavery, so my ears remained whole. The apostle Paul's description of a 'woman's crowning glory' decreed that my hair remained long. That same Paul declared that my crowning glory must be covered by a hat for church – and the nearest I got to wearing makeup was colouring my lips, in the haven of my bedroom, with a red Smartie.

Paul (my brother, not that pesky apostle) got a job in a children's wear firm. My mother was delighted when he brought home some sample clothes for me. I was no less pleased. These garments were BRAND NEW and a bit fashionable too.

Amongst them was a pair of smart blue trousers. Trousers – for a girl! My father was outraged. His daughter was never, ever, ever going to wear trousers. A verse from Deuteronomy was invoked: *'A woman must not put on men's clothing, and a man must not wear women's clothing. Anyone who does this is detestable in the sight of the LORD your God.* My tears were copious but my father stood firm.

70

Straightway, my mother spake. And lo, her words overruled Scripture! The blue trousers became a beloved addition to my wardrobe.

Trousers became de rigueur
after The Great Debate.
Just as well!

Work for idle hands

There were five days on five occasions in the year when my brothers sat still. And my mother hated it.

They sat in a row in the kitchen. They listened to the slow, low voice of John Arlott and the quick, light voice of Brian Johnston delivering the ball-by-ball commentary on Test Match Special on the BBC Third Programme. We ate when the cricketeers took their meals and my mother scrubbed and cooked and humphed around the large lumps of listening lads.

Not for long were they allowed to remain idle! Africa was suddenly inundated with piles of blankets made from knitted squares. John and Brian wittered on, but now their words were accompanied by the clack of needles. My mother had taught my brothers to knit.

Out for the count

My brother Daniel was obsessed by cricket. My brother Stephen was obsessed by numbers. A winning combination. There was a lot of time to fill between Test Match broadcasts. Adopting a continent each, my brothers played out their own cricket test matches over the intervening weeks. Stephen still has the number-crammed notebooks full of the statistics he created from their sporting battles. Wins, losses, draws, batting and bowling averages for both individual players and for teams... everything was recorded and analysed.

Me batting in a game of carpet cricket – a safer,
but arguably less exciting form of 'the gentleman's game'.

A good occupation for two boys playing cricket in the street or park, but Glasgow weather being what it was, most of the games took place in their bedroom. With a proper bat. And a proper cricket ball. When the tell-tale thud of leather on willow betrayed them, my parents would remonstrate and the cricket ball would be confiscated. Again.

Consigning the hard ball to my mother's hatbox proved little challenge to my brothers' determined searching. After a few days of sub-standard cricket with a tennis ball, the thwacks would resume. Sometimes a windowpane would be cracked – and the ball would be returned to the hatbox. Again.

After a decent interval, the ball was invariably brought back into play, and the matches resumed. There was no end to the ingenuity of the cricketing zealots. There were three beds in their room, as well as chests of drawers, a wardrobe and a bookcase. Space was tight; skill was required for the bowler to send down a ball with just enough force to offer challenge to the batsman who, in turn, must judge finely how hard he dare hit the ball. The beds, you see, acted as fielders. You were caught out if you hit the ball onto a bed and it stayed there.

Apart from the inconvenient fragility of glass windows, there were other obstacles too. Paul was now an apprentice piano tuner. Sometimes he brought home a whole piano action to work on. It was placed carefully on the bedroom mantelpiece, each piece numbered to ensure its correct positioning.

A cricket ball could play havoc with that. In the grand scheme of things, losing the Ashes was small beer.

O-T-T

In the summer holidays, when the boys were in their teens, we often ate our meals in the sitting room. How posh, you might think. But actually, it was because there was no table in the kitchen. Once school was out, our two tables were butted up together in the sitting room, a net was fixed between them, and the table tennis season began.

Probably my mother was able to thole the endless plick-plack of plastic ball on wooden bat because her teenage children were safely occupied playing a harmless, inexpensive game through the long weeks off school. Harmless maybe, but it was played in deadly earnest. Any spare player perched at the top of our paint-bespattered stepladder and refereed rigorously for the others. Just like Wimbledon really.

Special rules had to be created to allow for the 'squink' – the hinge line along the kitchen table created by raising the flap to bring its width nearer to that of the other table. As one table was oval and the two tables were not of equal lengths, skilled judgement both on and off the table was crucial. Many quarrels ensued. TT balls were fragile and, after some of the more ill-natured disputes, a bowl of warm water might be seen in the kitchen nursing the dents out of injured balls.

Much as I liked to play, opportunities for me to hone my TT skills were limited to times when no other opponent was available for one of my brothers. By this time, Paul had left school and now had a wage. His first major purchase was a tape recorder with which we had hours of fun. He was hardly likely to use his precious leisure time helping me to improve my table tennis but Stephen and Daniel could sometimes be kind...

'Want to come in and play TT?' they said one evening, smiling down on my eager, nine-year-old visage.

Game commenced and it was clear from the start that no quarter was to be given. So pleased was I to be invited to play, that I was careful to keep a stern grip on my emotions. Inside though, a little voice started up an insistent monologue; *if they'd just give me a chance, not serve so fast, not play to my weak side, not laugh when I missed...*

There's only so much defeat a little girl can take. I reached my limit and began to voice my feelings. The more noise I made, the more they laughed. The more they laughed, the less I could return the ball. I shouted, I screamed, I jumped, I hit the table, I roared. I was beaten on every front.

When I had reached the nadir of despair and the height of my expression of it, they threw open the door of the deep cupboard in the corner of the room.

Paul sat there grinning as he rewound the tape.

76

Ode to the vest

Sing out for the vest!
Much mocked and maligned.
A soft skin, clinging and caressing,
'neath garments picked for look more than feel.

Sing out for the vest!
Much mocked and maligned.
How will dignity survive
when threadbare fringes dim its gentle hems?

We all wore vests in the 1950s. The youngest and oldest of us wore the short-sleeved kind with fabric covered buttons down the front, while the middle of us wore them sleeveless with scooped-out fronts.

When a vest's days as a tender undergarment were over, it was not yet time for it to be cast aside. *Oh no no no!* Many honourable duties were still to come for the rest of the vest.

More lowly, more tattered vests might become the vehicle for spreading the white liquid clay on the tenement stairs as I gave them their weekly wash. How fresh and soft the vest felt at the top of the stairs; how sullied, caked and thick by the bottom.

Sometimes my mother invited me to help polish our lino

floors. Not much fun, you might think, down on your knees, scrubbing away. *Oh no no no!* You'd be quite wrong! First she washed the floors; next she tied a vest under each of my shoes; then she skimmed floor polish onto the vests. Now it was time for me to do my bit. Gliding and sliding, I skated our floors into a state of high gleam.

Polishing! Polishing! What finer job than polishing!

Some vests were raised to Even Higher Things. When our church (Victoria Place Baptist) closed down, my mother was invited to choose a gift to mark her years as organist there. In a moment of unwonted, unbridled desire, she asked for a pair of brass candlesticks.

Polishing! Polishing! What finer job than polishing!

What could be more splendid than to ease open the tin of Duraglit, draw out a bit of the moist fluffy fabric, scrub away on clouded metal and buff it up with a soft old vest? What greater satisfaction than to place the gleaming objects back on the mantelpiece and bask in their glow?

Brasses, brasses, oh bring on the brasses!

Mr Lewis kept the 'antique' shop in the next street. Small items of furniture jostled with vases, pre-war comic annuals, china vases, dingy landscapes… It was fun to look, and I often did. So it was that I saw a brass object which I knew my mother would love. Mr Lewis handed it over to me in exchange for seven shillings and sixpence. Heaven only knows how I raised a sum like that. That would be ten weeks' pocket money at ninepence a week and no sweets in all that time.

My mother was touched beyond words, though I suspect there might have been a little pucker at the corners of her mouth at the idea of her rather less than perfect daughter giving her a set of brass monkeys bidding all to 'Hear no evil, see no evil, speak no evil.'

Ah, Polishing! Polishing! What finer job than polishing!

Homemade entertainment

Mrs Farquarson was a big woman. Big in voice, big in stature, big in girth, big in largesse. Hailing from the Highlands, she and her husband John lived in Ibrox, as did many Clyde shipbuilding workers. And indeed, John was a carpenter with John Brown's Shipbuilders. With a good income and no family to spend it on, the Farquarsons could entertain in style. It may not have been 'stylish' but it was good, old-fashioned, Scottish hospitality and we loved it.

When we arrived for a visit, the front door was thrown open; we were enveloped in her smiles, her chins, her blooming cheeks, and above all, her glorious laugh which burbled and gurgled up from the moment she saw us. John was a mildish, smallish, gingerish, baldish, slightly surprised looking shadow whose role (apart from bringing home the bacon) seemed to be to echo and endorse, with many sucked-in breaths, many 'ayes' and many affirming head movements, the wonder, the veracity and the miraculous nature of Chrissie's endless supply of tales.

I can picture nothing about their kitchen except the table – the table which seemed to fill the room with its glorious munificence. We speak of tables which 'groan with goodies'. There was no groaning here. This table exulted in its burden. It delighted in flaunting its treasures as they sparkled and glistened and gleamed before our hungry eyes – and all set off by fine white napery. Butter (not Echo margarine) glowed gold on little china dishes, breads, meats, cheeses, homemade jams, homemade scones, homemade pancakes, homemade cake all jostled for our custom. Best of all, there was as much of anything as you wanted – not one item for each family member, as at my own family's humble table.

Over all this banquet our genial hostess presided with stories and laughter, her eyes twinkling behind little round glasses, her wavy, grey highland hair wisping out from her bun, her ample bosom straining at her pinny. How she attained her generous proportions was a mystery. She barely had time to sip her tea; her mouth had so many other duties.

Every coin has two sides. The Farquarson home had two public rooms. The kitchen was so full of light and joy that I was all but dazzled out of my appetite. But I knew that when the eating was over, we would be urged to come through to the Front Room.

The Front Room was cold and dark and still. Around the fireplace was a semicircle of chairs. Quite comfy, you might think. But we were not to sit upon those chairs. These were to lean upon as we knelt to pray. It seemed that the longer we sat at the kitchen table, the longer we must then spend on our knees. Mrs Farquarson loved her food but not as much as she loved her Lord. Her wanton laughter was screwed away in a storage jar in the kitchen and a highland lugubriousness unstoppered in the Front Room. Each phrase of her conversation with her unseen Master began with, and was punctuated by, drawn-in oooohing sighs, and each ended with a long exhalation. It made for slow progress. Of course each adult must chip in contributions to the human side of this exchange – and not just once. Just when it would seem to be over, one of the kneelers would think of another needy soul to be lifted up before the Lord – or another blessing for which to offer mournful thanks.

It happened that Mrs Farquarson (though a member of the Free Church and not a believer in the use of musical instruments in church) played and owned a fine concertina, a lovely piece of gleaming silver and polished leather. It happened that Mrs Farquarson had invited another family with a little girl to join us for tea that day. It happened that during the interminable prayer session, Moira and I got our hands on the concertina. (Of course there was not an eye open among the fervent, grown-up pray-ers.) It happened that we two lasses were equally stubborn about letting go of the concertina so that the other could examine it more closely.

It happened. With a sickening wrench, the bellows ripped apart and, no doubt, our stomachs with it.

Live coals

Lighting the fire was my father's job. Before we enjoyed the benefit of a 'gas poker', it could be quite a job, too – depending on how the wind was blowing. It was not uncommon to see my father down on his knees puffing the embers into life, or holding a double spread of the News Chronicle in front of the whole opening to get the fire to draw. Sometimes my father, inveterate reader that he was, became caught up in some article in the paper spread before him and the whole sheet would catch fire and have to be hastily pokered down into the grate.

When I need a safe place to go in my mind, that kitchen fire is always there. Its warmth, its light, its shifting shapes and colours were the heart empowering the family life that went on around it. I sat before that fire on the hearthrug and dreamed, watching molten caves appear and vanish within it; I played there in my nightclothes, dropping buttons through the hole in the top of a little stool while its heat dried my newly-washed hair; I held a toasting fork close to it on Sundays to make cinnamon toast for tea.

Sometimes one or both parents would be in their armchairs right beside me, reading or sewing. All of us sat enthralled around the fire as my father read *The Pilgrim's*

Progress and *The Swiss Family Robinson* aloud to us.

When I was older, I joined the others to listen to the Ten O'clock News there. We were sitting right there in front of the fire on the night we heard that President Kennedy had been shot.

Pollokshields, Glasgow

age 10–12

At the hub

When I look at this photograph of Paul with my mother in our kitchen, I realise that the pictures in my head which have shaped the words I have written focus on the actual living that went on in our household. Nothing of the dinginess of our home clouds my mind's eye. As I recall the familiar objects in this photograph, I find that my memories of them are bound up with their significance, rather than their intrinsic qualities.

My mother is pouring tea from a 'Judge' enamel teapot.

The knob on the top of the lid bore the embossed head of a judge with a curly wig; I can feel the shape under my fingers now. The smoked glass tumbler on the left of the table was one of a set which Paul won at the Kelvin Hall Carnival. Probably the cups and saucers were one of his purchases. He loved a bargain. He still does.

In a time before formica swept over the nation's kitchens, our table is covered by sticky-backed Fablon to make the surface easy to keep clean. It was the very dickens to apply without bubbles appearing – bubbles which we, rather missing the point, later poked with our forks or fingernails, allowing moisture and dirt to creep underneath.

Behind Paul is one of the two armchairs which flanked the coal fire, where my mother would sit to darn and my father to read. On the seat of the chair is one of many cosy rugs of colourful, crocheted squares, sewn together and edged in more crochet, which my mother seemed to conjure up in her 'spare time'.

The coal fire heated the water too and there was a wooden-cased hot water tank above the rather misshapen pipe which can be seen in the corner. The scorch mark on the wall may be related to a memorable Sunday when my brother enthusiastically banked up a massive blaze in the grate. My parents had been keeping the fire low as the chimney sweep was due to come next day for a much-needed visit. Despite the fire engine's flamboyant arrival in our street, we were still packed off to Sunday School and missed the whole show.

The rather incongruously grand case of cutlery open on top of the 'larder' (no fridge of course) was a wedding present to my parents. Its contents were in daily use. The long curtain is restrained by the rope from the ever-used and ever-useful pulley. One might question the need for a lace curtain when we lived one floor up with two back greens between us and the houses opposite. But my mother was scathing of bare windows – as if an undressed window was somehow indecent.

I am struck by the emptiness of the undersink area where most of us store our army of cleaning agents. Steel wool, Ajax, and not much else seem to be my mother's weapons against the germs she constantly battled; the soap dish and nail brush hooked onto the window shutter ensured our clean hands. Against the general greyness visible in the photo, the sink itself gleams out. It was a shiny new stainless steel affair, much anticipated by my mother. Dare I say of someone so unworldly that she was even a little proud of it?

Looking at the people in the picture, I like my mother's quiet smile as she ministers to her son. As for Paul, I have no pictures of him taken at home when he is not holding a cat.

Finger exercises

We all four learned to play the piano. It was just what we did. Depending on our differing temperaments, we were more or less conscientious about doing the work set by our piano teacher. But we all *played* the piano, most of us a lot. Except when our downstairs neighbour had had enough. Then her daughter would come up and report that her long-suffering mother had a headache and could we please not exarcebate it by playing piano, violins, flute or singing – all of which we did rather more than even the most ardent music-loving neighbour could want.

We didn't always have a piano in our house. In

Bridgeton, my mother bought a harmonium (or American organ) from a local second-hand shop and gave us our first lessons. You had to work the pedals up and down to make the sound. If you were as little as I was, it was difficult to sit low enough to pump in air with your feet while still sitting high enough to have your hands on the keys and your eyes on the music.

When we moved to Pollokshields, we got a real piano and were sent to lessons with Miss Mabel Ballantyne LRAM. At half-a-crown a lesson for each of us, Miss Ballantyne was never going to be rich, but ten shillings a week was a big outlay for my parents. I like to think that we made good use of it. Whether it was despite, or because of the lessons, two of us have made our living from the piano: I as a piano teacher, and Paul as a piano tuner and light music pianist. Paul might give a wry smile at the memory of his piano lessons; he was assuredly the one of us who brought the least pleasure to our piano teacher. Yet he is the one who has spent his life bringing pleasure to so many through his own beguiling style of piano playing.

I often reflect on my feeling of dread as I pulled Miss Ballantyne's jangling brass bell and my forlorn hope that this week she would not be there. But of course she was always there – no teaching, no money. As I stood waiting for her to open the door to me, I made fervent, internal vows that next week would be different. I would be well-prepared and would stand there with pride and pleasant anticipation.

Actually, she was perfectly agreeable: no rapping of fingers with rulers, or shouting at lazy pupils. No, she smiled, took an interest in us and prepared us, whether we liked it or not, for exams. I enjoyed all music-making but I was not very good at getting down to the serious practice required for exams. Still, the weekly lesson improved my ability to read music at sight as I tried to conceal my lack of preparation.

Miss Ballantyne taught in a small room on a large, grand piano. There was just room for the pupil's stool, the teacher's chair, a chair for the next pupil and a cabinet of music. A low coal fire was always burning and her two black-and-white cats, Binkie and Paddy, luxuriated on a rug before it or gazed out of the window at the world beyond.

It was through Binkie and Paddy that our relationship with Miss Ballantyne developed beyond piano lessons. When she went on holiday, we fed her cats. Nothing untoward in that, although we did have to walk a mile each way to do it.

Feeding the cats and cleaning their ash-litter tray meant that we had to go into other rooms in the house. The music room could not have been described as plush, elegant or comfortable. Fit for purpose was as generous as one could be. So, how to describe the rest of the house? The bathroom, where the litter tray resided, boasted a dark green painted bath and yes, coal really *was* stored in it. In the kitchen, there were bare floor boards. I'm not talking trendy, sanded and varnished boards; these were grey and dusty and between them lived… a colony, a continent, a galaxy of fleas, all ready and waiting to feed on our fresh, young flesh.

My mother's nursing background ensured that, though we might be shabby, we were clean – clean to our skins. The only time I heard my mother breath a divine imprecation was when she found lice in my waist-length hair. Much distempering, papering and painting of rooms went on in our house. My mother, old clothes bespattered, head tied in a cloth (distemper was messy stuff to attach to a ceiling), would stand back and survey her work. 'At least,' she would sniff, 'it's clean.' So sending her children to a house teeming with bloodsucking parasites must have seemed to her as if she were sending them, unprotected, into Elm Street.

Paul, wearing the much needed headgear,
while distempering the ceiling

We developed a technique. A large bowl of salted water was left inside the front door of Miss Ballantyne's house. After a hasty dash to deal with the needs of both ends of the cats, we picked the marauding, pesky blighters off our skin as we left the house and dropped them into the water. Further grooming took place when we got home.

A mystery remains. Where did the fleas go for the rest of the year?

A peasouper

My mother was born and bred in London. My father moved there from Manchester in his 20's. For me, London was where it was at! London had the Blitz. London had the Queen. London had Big Ben. London had Winston Churchill. London had 'peasoupers'.

Shoes tell a story in Trafalgar Square. The stylish sandals belong to Auntie Janet. The less glamorous one at the edge of the picture belongs to my mother. The pigeons are well placed to conceal the hole in the toe of my right sandal.

I never tired of hearing about London and I loved to visit my aunt there, even though the bus journey took 16 hours and I began being sick before we reached the outskirts of Glasgow.

Once, my brothers made the trip themselves during the Christmas holidays. They look about nine, eleven and thirteen in the jolly picture of them in Trafalgar Square with my aunt in her cosy, fur coat. On the way out of London, with visibility hampered by a peasouper, their bus came off the road. Sixteen hours stretched to many more but they were unhurt and had a good story to tell.

The very name 'peasouper' enchanted me. Was it really possible that you could, as my mother averred, hold up your hand in front of you in the street and not be able to count your fingers? Oh, London had it all.

Of course, in those days when coal warmed all our houses and ran our factories, Glasgow had its share of fog too. Unaware, or perhaps all too aware, of its dangers, I was fascinated by it. In the fog, our neighbourhood became a place of mystery, intrigue and possibility. So, on a particularly foggy day after school, I, aged ten, was quite gung ho about setting off alone as usual on the mile-long walk to my piano lesson. Perhaps to enhance the danger, I chose a quiet route rather than going along the busier streets with their lit shops.

It was all as I had imagined it would be. The mists swirled around me, infiltrating my nose and throat; sound (such as there was) was dulled; even the light from the street lamps was muffled and diffuse; and yes – I held up my mittened hand – I could not see my hand before me, never mind count my fingers. It was the real thing! I was in a peasouper!

I missed my piano lesson that day. I missed all the local landmarks. I could not believe that I could become hopelessly, helplessly lost in the familiar streets near my home. I wandered for a long time, turning every which way and becoming just a *little* worried and scared, though it was still a bit of an adventure. My brother had been sent out to look for me but our paths did not cross – or if they did, we hadn't noticed. I was saved by the dim cigarette advertisement light above Brown's newsagent. The little shop appeared to be standing alone like a general store in a one-horse US town.

I reached the newsagents but of course my journey wasn't over. I took my bearings and headed the half mile home.

Give a little whistle

Windows afford more than light! There are places in Glasgow where people keep a cushion on the window sill. That way, they can interact with the world, their elbows resting comfortably rather than being rasped raw by rough stone.

Mrs Barr was an invalid lady who lived in a ground-floor flat in my street. She seldom left her bed which was placed right at the front window so that she could see and remark on everything that passed by. If you wanted to know anything about the neighbours, you would ask Mrs Barr. She knew much more than you would want to know, possibly more than there was to know...

Of course my mother had neither time nor inclination to hang out of windows – not unless one of us was late home. As I urged my tardy feet along our street, my eyes would be fixed from afar on our front windows. Would the irate little head be bobbing there and the peremptory beckoning hand be urging me on? Had I timed my return just late enough for only a mild scolding? If the head was there, I had not.

Stephen and I at the front window.
How else do you shake the dust off the wall brush?

My bedroom window was at the back of the house. On light summer evenings when it felt too early to be in bed, I would slide open the sash so that I could look at, listen to, and smell, the outside world. No cushion softened the ledge but I liked to see and feel the stone sill and watch the busy bustling of tiny insects there. Looking beyond, I could see into the back greens of at least six tenements – more, if I cared to lean dangerously far out. Two or three had large trees. Being one floor up, I could see right into the world of their branches and leaves.

On the top of one tree, a blackbird sang his evening praise, night after night. Oh, the trills and frills he produced for my delight. He seemed to be waiting for an answer. Shall I give it a go? My whistle pierced the air.

Strong but unsubtle. I listened again, his song so stirring, so untrammelled. I tried to match his cadence.

Soon, we sang a nightly duet. He led, he was always full of ideas. I followed, I answered, a pale copy of his joyous glory.

Nightlife

My adult children joke that they can contact me at any time of the night and I will be awake, ready to answer their call. When I go to visit them, they leave me to shut down their houses long after they are tucked up in bed. The truth is, it was ever thus for me.

However much I fought against being sent to bed, there were many consolations once I got there. Sleep was still another life away. Of course I read until my light was turned out. Of course I read with a torch until the batteries yielded their last grain of power. Of course I turned my light on again after my parents were in bed. I read lying on my tummy, chin resting on my elbows, biting my nails. My book lay open on the pillow before me, spare one at the ready beneath the pillow. I read until I could not hold my eyes open another instant. Then I slept. When I woke in the morning, I read again.

For a little light relief before the night's reading began, if I happened to have some Midget Gems, I might play out a game of 'houses' or 'schools,' lining up the sweets on my sheet, grouping them in families of colours or shapes and rearranging them to meet the needs of the storyline. There was a natural limit to this pursuit, I admit, as I gradually ate my way through the participants.

Between the time of 'official lights out' and 'unofficial lights back on', I and Rupert, my bear, conducted our life together in a parallel universe in a tent under the bedclothes. In that world, my name was Doris and I had golden curls. That was the extent of the glamour bit. Most of our adventures involved rescuing unwanted children from unimaginable dangers and then adopting them into our rambling, tent-based family.

I had heard of someone being described as 'a light sleeper'. I liked that phrase. That was me. I adopted it and used it whenever I could. The light sleeper could be easily disturbed by the any small stirrings about the house. That explained why I was awake as soon as anyone was afoot.

It was no 'small stirring' when the 'midgie-men' made their weekly visit. They tramped through the closes in the dead of night to empty the great metal middens full of vegetable peelings and ashes, housed by the back wall of the back green. They shouted and laughed and banged about as if it were bright day. 'Light sleeper' that I was, I was up and out of bed as soon as I heard the first crash. The men wore head torches which lit up the back green in meteor-like streaks, ever shifting, overlapping, swooping. I would stand at my window, watching, watching until the unbroken darkness and silence returned.

Laugh and the world laughs with you

L ooking at this photograph, you would know right away that Daniel (second from right) was a giggler. Wide, toothy grin, shoulders up and he was away. It was as easy to set him off as it was hard to stop him, and once Daniel started giggling, my mother wasn't far behind.

At the annual Sunday School prizegiving, the children sat in the front rows of the church flanked by their teachers, who were strategically positioned to separate potentially troublesome children. Our mother, one of those teachers, placed Daniel right beside her, 'where I can keep an eye on you', she had no doubt said.

From my place in the pew behind, I saw it all. Daniel's shoulders rose and fell, rose and fell. My mother wore the strangest expression, her cheeks sucked in as if she was holding a mouthful of lemon juice, her face reddening as I watched in alarm.

By now, Daniel's shoulders were shaking uncontrollably and – good heavens! – so were my mother's. Soundlessly they writhed and squirmed as if a host of earwigs roamed over their bodies. Ere long it was over. They – and I – slumped back in limp relief.

But what on earth was so funny?

ⓒ

Neighbours

If you look again at the picture in the previous story, you will see chicken wire fixed to the window bars of the ground floor flat. Mr and Mrs Brown, whose flat it was, put it there to stop our cat visiting their house when their windows were open.

Mr and Mrs Brown had much to put up with from their upstairs neighbours, the Cohens. There were the clumping feet of three big boys; there was the relentless banging on the piano, the screeching of violins, and the singing too; there was the daughter ceaselessly throwing balls against the landing wall to the rhythm of the ditties she sang. And even if the Cohen's cat could no longer pop in to their house, it still did its business in the little border of roses outside their kitchen window that Mr Brown tended so lovingly. Yes, it was tough living below the Cohens.

Mr and Mrs Brown might have wished for a quieter life, but we all got on as good neighbours should, helping out when needed and remaining on friendly terms.

Mr and Mrs Brown had two daughters. I was five years older than Belinda and five years younger than Lesley. You might say that there was a hierarchy of admiration between us. As I looked up to Lesley, so Belinda looked up to me.

She loved to tag behind me, play with me, walk down to Woolworths in Paisley Road with me.

Sometimes I kept her company when her parents were out; my mother was always upstairs if needed. Having short hair herself, Belinda was enchanted by my long locks and delighted in playing with them. We would sit on the couch together and chatter away while she brushed my hair.

Usually Belinda was not short of chat, so I was surprised, on one such occasion, to notice that I was doing all the talking and receiving only occasional monosyllables in reply.

ME: What's wrong, Belinda?

BELINDA [*quickly*]: Nothing. I'm fine

ME: You're awfully quiet. Are you sure you're okay?

BELINDA [*quickly*]: I'm fine, honest.

ME: Are you annoyed about someth—owww

BELINDA: Sorry, I didn't mean to hurt you.

ME: Owww, owww, o-o-o-o-w-w-w! What are you doing to my hair?

BELINDA: Sorry I'll be more caref—

ME: Owww, owww! What on earth are you doing?

BELINDA [*slowly*]: I might just have caught the brush in your hair a bit.

ME [*briskly*]: Oh, give it to me. I'll get it out. You just need to turn the brush the other way.

[tries to unroll the hair from the brush without success]

ME [*forlornly*]: Maybe you'd better do it. At least you can see what you're doing.

Belinda turned the brush this way and that, trying to free my imprisoned tresses. I turned myself this way and that, trying to relieve the tug of each hair being stretched to and beyond its limit.

At length(!), the brush reached an impasse, its bristles pressed hard against my head. We were both distraught. I fled upstairs to call my mother. She would know what to do. She would sort it.

She did indeed. It took a long time to regrow the clump that she chopped off an inch from my skull.

New neighbours

The flats in Pollokshields were big and roomy. The streets nearest to the trading sector of the city were a bit less smart and the properties a bit less pricey. Perhaps for these three reasons, size, location and price, the flats in McCulloch Street where we lived were an attractive option for immigrant families.

Around the mid-1950s, the first arrivals from Pakistan moved into our street. Great Britain was not then the multicultural melting pot that it has since become. Most of our knowledge of people from 'overseas' was gleaned from books – and from missionary slide shows. It would be unthinkable to repeat the words of people from such a different era; enough to say that the locals were wary and not a little nervous at the prospect of the arrival of a more cosmopolitan populace.

The flat across the landing from ours had become vacant and, when we heard the surname of the family who were to move in, there was some muttered consternation amongst some of our neighbours. My parents were calm and welcoming. After all, quite apart from their Christian principles, it was only sixty or so years since my father's family had arrived in Britain from Lithuania with no money, no English and few useful skills.

Our new neighbours moved in. There were four little boys and a baby on the way. Everybody was smiley and well-disposed. It wasn't long before the two oldest boys were visiting our house for help with their English homework and I was visiting theirs to help look after the small brothers.

Pictured below is Jaswant, the oldest boy, reading a giant book about fairies with me. He and I were best friends until they moved on – to a nicer house in a nicer area.

Health and Safety

C hurch, if I have not already made this clear, was obligatory. Twice on Sunday. And Sunday School in the afternoon in between. You had to be VERY UNWELL INDEED to be allowed to miss any of these.

I was very unwell indeed and this raised a dilemma. My mother was the church organist so she couldn't stay at home with me. My father must have had deaconly duties that day, or perhaps he was preaching elsewhere. He certainly was not able stay at home. At seventeen, my brother Paul was a church organist too so he couldn't stay at home. Leaving one of the other brothers with me might be more of a threat to my safety than leaving me on my own. And they would miss getting their Young Worshippers' League card stamped and that would lose them their 'perfect attendance' status.

Anyway, *being ill* meant being *in bed*. What harm could I come to? I was left at home that Sunday morning with stern injunctions to stay in bed. And I did; I dozed for a bit, I read for a bit, I wondered what else I could do.

I had recently been given a yellow bedside lamp which had a porcelain vase-shaped base, very smooth to the touch, and with a pleated shade. I enjoyed stroking both textures for a while. Somehow the light fitting got a bit loose from the base. Better tighten it up by turning the fitting... and turning it a bit more... oops, where did that metal nut come from that just dropped out of the base?... now the fitting seems to be even looser... better twist it a bit more.

Did I mention that the light was switched on? Not any more, actually. There was a bit of extra brilliance and a bang before it went out.

What harm could I come to in bed?

Doctor's call

Stephen was asthmatic. Dr Cowan, whose surgery was in Bridgeton, continued to attend our family when we moved to Pollokshields. He was 'good with Stephen', you see. He seemed happy to make the five-mile journey when required. Without antibiotics and inhalers, it was required quite often.

It was a good job that Stephen was clever because he spent a lot of time off school and in bed. Mind you, he did find things to do in bed apart from wheezing and reading. When my mother came to straighten up his bed before the doctor's visit, she had a bit of a problem with some tiny red stones rolling about in his sheets. Stephen had been having a bit of a problem with them too. It might have been easy to get the 17 jewels out of his watch but...

Wheezing may not have been fun, but days off school were always welcome, as was a bit of extra parental care and attention. Sometimes a fire would be lit in the sickroom – the last word in luxury! So it wasn't surprising that I might want to develop an ailment or two of my own. I'd had my share of days in bed with my grumbling tonsils, but once they had been removed, new disorders were required.

I had sore knees. I really did. Sore heels too. Maybe, I

111

was growing at last. Anyway, as Dr Cowan was making the trip across Glasgow to visit Stephen yet again, it was decided to ask if he would look me over too. To save him making the trip all the way across the hall to my room, I was popped into one of my brother's beds.

I saw his jaunty bow tie arrive, heard his grave murmurings over Stephen and awaited his ministrations. My mother described my pains and pulled back the covers for him to examine my knees. Stephen was fair-skinned and pale. I was sallow-skinned and brown. The great doctor barely glanced. 'Nothing wrong with her but dirt,' he snorted and swept on.

B*****

June 25th 1917 / Yours Sincerely Eli Cohen.

T here was no swearing in our house. There was No Swearing in our house. Maybe I sensed a sotto voce sh** from a bold teenage brother once or twice, but there was NO SWEARING in our house. Mind, I did witness my father knocking on the window at cats fighting on the wash-house roof. 'Gerraway yuh liddle beggars,' he shouted in his slow Lancashire voice; then his head drooped in remorse. 'Learned it in the army,' he muttered and I was left to wonder what was so foul-mouthed about 'beggars'.

In truth, I had no desire to swear. It just didn't appeal to me. But when I cut my finger spreading my toast, I seized the chance. 'Take that bloody margarine away,' I ventured.

The parents descended like eagles on a helpless lamb. I pointed wordlessly to the drop of my life blood smeared on the Echo margarine wrapper.

A small, if pyrrhic, victory.

A lot of learning

My mother didn't have a paid job though she was a trained nurse. Bringing up the family and being the hostess of a mission house was pretty labour-intensive. Making a missionary's stipend meet all the ends that four children demanded required skill and ingenuity. Being family seamstress, church organist and choirmistress, as well as friend and helper to all those less fortunate than we were, lent variety and challenge to her days. Why then, should she would want to take on an allotment as well was beyond us. Something to do with growing boys and sacks of potatoes, I think.

The 'plot', as we called it, was in the New Victoria Gardens, five minutes walk from our house. Its high railings and hedges screened from the general public the realisation of many a city man's dream of country living. Each allotment boasted some sort of greenhouse; most were creatively fashioned from old windows, doors, pallets or scrap metal. It was against the creed of the place to buy anything new and that suited my parents just fine. What wasn't so fine for them was the rule that at least one-third of the ground must be used for growing flowers when my parents intended to grow only vegetables.

It was fine for me though. I loved flowers. I delighted in learning their names and in learning how best they could be coaxed to grow. I spent many hours looking over people's hedges and watching them work or take their ease amongst their flora. I learned that people who enjoy gardening are lovely people. Or perhaps it is lovely people who enjoy gardening? Whichever, there was an atmosphere of calm, of co-operation, and of quiet content in the air. Friendships blossomed as much as flowers, and often between members of differing generations and sectors of the population.

Admittedly, the Annual Flower and Produce Show placed a strain on those bonds of friendship. Competition was fierce and judging meticulous, with the appearance, size, shape and taste of the vegetables being minutely scrutinised. Children were urged into the fray, making arrangements of pressed pansies stuck on boards or miniature gardens nestling in soup plates.

It was fun to walk round the gardens after the judging and see the prize cards shouting from stakes in the winning gardens. Had Mr Brock with the friendly black-and-white spaniel carried off first prize yet again for his herbaceous border, his dahlias, his chrysanthemums, his roses...? I learned in those days a truth I have confirmed since. Men who garden are concerned with doing things right, doing things in lines – and growing the biggest.

My parents were not skilled or experienced gardeners, but despite their children's reluctance to dig and weed, we harvested potatoes, leeks, cabbages and other fine vegetables; our greenhouse redolated with the wonderful smell of fresh tomatoes, and our leafy rhubarb patch produced a forest of juicy stems. Nothing quite quenched one's appetite for sweet and sour like a thin stalk of rhubarb dipped in a paper cone of sugar.

Our flourishing plot. The green card waving on a stake in front of the centre pane of the of the greenhouse is our only ever award in the Annual Show: Third Prize for our cabbages!

So, my parents learned how to cultivate fine vegetables. We all learned to go the long way home when bearing flowers. If we went the short way, we would pass my little friend, Kaneez. She would fix her soulful dark eyes on the flowers and soon they would be in her arms.

My brothers learned that spinach, our least favourite vegetable, grows bigger and better the more you trample on it, and I learned that, despite my best ministrations, noodles, when planted, do not grow at all.

Temptation

M y mother's store cupboard was slender but there was always flour stored in National Dried Milk tins, little containers of cinnamon and nutmeg, and usually jars of sultanas, currants, raisins and coconut. When pining for a taste of exotic sweetness, I would filch little handfuls of the last two and mix them with dry Puffed Wheat.

Less often, there were dates, syrup and cocoa, all of which promised rare and tasty titbits. And of course there were raising agents for scones and cakes: baking powder, cream of tartar, and bicarbonate of soda which, as everyone knew, was also useful for putting on burns.

There was one small jar which fascinated me with the bright red glow of its contents. I'd sampled most things in the cupboard with more or less pleasing results but my mother had warned me that I should not give in to the tempting allure of those blush-red pods.

Looking for a novel nibble, I considered the roseate jar once more. I knew I should heed my mother's words. But then again, it was not so long since she had told me that if I ate any of the chocolates hanging on the Christmas tree before 25 December, she would know because I would be sick. Maybe the tale of purported danger lurking in the red jar was just such another ruse to warn me off. One taste couldn't be too awful, I reasoned, and one pod missing would surely not be noticed.

It would not have been so bad if I'd only licked the dried chilli, but I bit right in and my mouth exploded. No amount of bicarbonate of soda could soothe my scarlet, swollen lips.

The cost of obedience

M other's Day was a new commercial opportunity in Britain in the 1950s but it was catching on fast. When I was ten, we made flower-decorated cards on the last Friday afternoon of March to give to our mothers on that special Sunday. Ever humble, my mother was not in favour of a day devoted to fêting her, though I daresay a little uncomplaining help with table-setting and dish-washing would have been mighty welcome.

My friends were buying presents for their mothers – flowers, toffees, nice things. Timidly, I asked my mother what might be an acceptable present. Fulsome in her determination not to add another financial commitment onto her children's slight means, she was dismissive. 'I want nothing,' she declared. As if to emphasise her point, she tucked her straying hair back into her little bun; 'nothing but a packet of hairpins.'

Obedience was often challenging for me, but this time I could do it! I bought a packet of hairpins and presented them to my mother on Mother's Day. And wouldn't you know, she was playing the piano for Sunday School that very day! Nice, dainty, prim Miss Watt asked us if we knew what special day it was. 'Mother's Day,' we chorused, surprised to be asked a question to which the was something other than 'God' or 'Jesus' or 'The Bible'.

It was perfectly natural for Miss Watt to ask *my* mother, as the only mother there, what gifts she had received that morning. Perhaps my mother regretted her words afterwards. Perhaps I'd have felt vindicated had she ranted on about commercial exploitation. No doubt the words tripped off her tongue without a thought.

She said, 'Nothing but a packet of hairpins.'

Monkey business

My mother managed the household money with prudence and rigour. In my mother's drawer in the kitchen were the tools of the thrifty housewife. There was her purse for the daily shopping; there was a tin which held the week's housekeeping (including our pocket money and piano lesson fees); there was an accounts book where she noted every transaction of the week; and there was the Treasury Box.

All money which came into our house was tithed – except for personal gifts to the children. The Treasury Box held the tithed money; it covered our collections for church services and any donations to charities. My mother's attitude to the family finances was well illustrated by her choice of money containers. The week's housekeeping money was kept in an Elastoplast tin. The Treasury money reposed in a lovely circular box which looked to be made of ivory.

We were allowed to accept gifts of money from visitors or relatives. But it was a basic rule of life that to help others was a joyful service bringing its own reward; so if we ran errands or did chores for people, we knew we should not accept money.

All life seemed to happen to me on the road to and from

my piano lesson. As I fought my way home on a wild windy afternoon, an old lady popped her head out of a close and asked me to go to the shops for her.

A good deed, I thought, *I'm doing a good deed!* (By this time I was an earnest Girl Guide). I felt important, responsible – righteous even – as I staggered through the harsh elements to bring the essentials of life to this weaker fellow human. I returned with the shopping to the lady's thanks and the injunction that I 'keep the change'. No, no, I demurred. The whole import of my selfless act would be lost were it to be tarnished with a mercenary aspect.

She was pressing, I stood firm; she was more pressing, I began to waver; she insisted, I gave in. No mess of pottage could have been more bitter. The sweets I spent the money on tasted as dust in my weak, fickle mouth.

Margaret, my friend across the road, had a cheery grandad who always seemed to enjoy our high spirits and silliness. I took over my musical box to entertain him. Decorated like a barrel organ, it played *Le Carnaval de Venise* and as I turned the handle on the side, a monkey in red jacket and fez bobbed up and down on the top. Margaret's grandad was charmed, as I'd hoped. He told me that organ grinders used to play in the street for money and he declared that he must pay me for playing to him. I was horrified when he held out three big coppers to me and I steadfastly refused to accept them. 'Oh well,' he said 'I'll put them here on the mantelpiece. But I have to warn you that the longer they stay there, the more they'll grow.'

Each time Margaret and I returned to the kitchen where he sat, the pile was one coin higher. Each time he pointed to the stack, I reiterated my resolve not to take his money. By the time the pile was ten coins high, I was becoming alarmed. What could I do? If I didn't accept the money soon, this sweet old man would be bankrupt. It was a positive kindness on my part to give in – and the sooner the better.

Murmuring my thanks, I put the pile of pennies in my pocket.

Ladies

C hurch was a haven for single ladies who were not in
the first flush of youth. In many respects, such ladies
ran the church. They made the tea, they manned the Sunday
School, they cleaned the building, they kept registers, they
ran mid-week meetings... They could be relied upon to do
whatever was needed.

Miss Black was one such; she was also a sweet friend to
me. Perhaps, having no children of her own, she appreciated
young company. She often invited me and my friend to tea
on Sundays before the evening service and it was always our
pleasure to accept.

She lived in a little two-apartment flat in Govanhill. The
paint and the brass fittings of her front door gleamed their
welcome to us, as did she. Miss Black treated us like ladies
and while there, we behaved like them too. The repast was
laid out charmingly on an embroidered cloth on a tea trolley.
We sat demurely on easy chairs in the kitchen while she
served us dainty morsels on delicate china. She listened to
our girl chatter, made pertinent comments and laughed
along with us. We dutifully washed and dried the dishes
afterwards and sat, chatting until it was time to leave
for church.

Well, almost time. There was still one thing more to do. Our lovely hostess with her perfect little home would take down the big key from where it hung by the front door and solemnly hold it out to us.

We knew what to do. Downstairs to the half landing, we would trot to where the shared toilet was situated. One of us would hand the key to the other who was waiting, then return upstairs to wash our hands at Miss Black's kitchen sink.

Dignity has nothing to do with riches.

A change is better than a rest

Mr and Mrs Silver invited me to stay with them and their three children in Carlisle. A 'converted' Jew, Mr Silver was a Church of England curate there. My parents knew the Silvers through the *Hebrew Christian Alliance*. They were happy to know that I would be in safe hands with these thoroughly Godly people.

I arrived on Saturday and spent the day getting to know the children. Sunday morning meant church of course; no change from home there, then. It was after Sunday dinner that I began to wonder if my parents really knew the people they had entrusted me to. The weather was fine and we children were shooed out into the garden to play. We could play chases, kick balls, skip – anything we liked really. Nothing so special there...

...but this was Sunday, for heaven's sake! The choice of activities open to my family on the Lord's Day in between the three church attendances was to go for a quiet walk or to stay at home and read. Oh sorry, I forgot – we could always play the 'History Game'. This was a kind of lotto in which the cards featured admirable characters from the past. The cards bore not just their names but an account of their lives and deeds. We were encouraged to read these potted histories while we waited for our turn. There was Florence Nightingale, Grace Darling, David Livingstone... oh, a host of fascinating worthies to inspire us to 'look up and aim high'.

Back in the garden in Carlisle, I hesitated to join in the frolics. What if my father telephoned to see how I was and they told him I was out playing? Surely he'd be on the first train down to collect me? Maybe I should phone home and pre-empt his discovery of my perfidy?

Still, we were having great fun. I found I got used to it quite quickly.

On the broad road

It was discovered in one of the regular school medical examinations that my hearing was a bit suspect. There followed many visits to many clinics. I was made to don alien-looking headphones and to report when I heard noises through them. It was only after the problem was solved (by having my ears syringed a few times) that I realised that the noises I so confidently reported hearing were the sounds of the dials and switches being operated to create the more subtle noises that I hadn't heard. When a train passed as I walked under a railway bridge after my ears had been cleared, I thought that the war, still so alive in adult conversation, had begun again.

My father, who worked afternoons and evenings, took me to these morning clinic appointments for which I had to forego some time at school. Not a minute more than absolutely necessary must be missed, so I had to go to school straight from the clinic. Walking in late to my classroom seemed to me like walking in naked to church. I always hoped to slip into the playground during morning break then go back to class as if I'd been there all the time.

Of course it couldn't always work out perfectly. The day came when my father left me to complete the journey back to school myself and I knew that I had missed break-time. With each dragging step along Melville Street towards my school, I pictured more graphically the approaching scene: the pupils lifting their heads from their work, the teacher asking me how I'd got on, the long walk from the front of the class to my seat at the back with all eyes on me.

Perhaps my words here don't fully capture the frightful situation I envisaged and the horror it engendered in me. A show-off I might be, shouting out answers in class, embarrassing my brothers by singing freely on buses and trams; but to walk into my familiar classroom in front of my familiar classmates and to respond to the pleasantries of my familiar teacher was to leave my comfort zone in another galaxy.

My sluggish feet reached the playground. Stomach rolling, heartbeats vibrating throughout my body, there was only the briefest of contests between *flight* and *fight* responses. I turned my steps away from the school. My heart did not stop pounding. I could not believe what I had done. Missing school for a good reason was an offence only a little below manslaughter. Deliberately avoiding school must rate close to murder which was, at that time, still a hanging offence.

The righteous reader will be satisfied to know that I derived no joy from my stateless situation. I lurked in the streets until I considered it the right time to go home for the dinner-break. As I neared my house, a new horror stabbed my overladen conscience. I was still bearing my satchel which should be safely residing under my desk. To return home with it was to advertise my guilt.

Oh, what a tangled web we weave / When first we practise to deceive! Surely the great Sir Walter Scott must, like me, have known what it was to skip school to have got it so right in his poem? The admonitions of a hundred Sunday School lessons battered my head. *One lie leads to another... be sure your sins will find you out...*

Was I a natural at deceit? Once I had quelled my panic, it was worryingly easy to solve this latest difficulty. When I reached my close, I walked straight through to the backgreen. I laid my satchel in a corner and covered it with handfuls of grass. I skipped upstairs, entered my home, ate my meal and left to return to school. I was a mite concerned about retrieving my school bag and being spotted carrying it back to school. Still believing myself to be at the centre of the universe, it seemed more than likely that I might be apprehended and challenged by some vigilant citizen or passing school-attendance officer. I slunk along, hiding my satchel as I passed people – people, who, in truth, probably didn't notice that furtive small girl, let alone entertain notions of her heinous offence.

My secret was never uncovered. But for those of you tempted to a life of crime, I must tell you that my sense of myself remained blighted until the more crimson deeds of grown-up life obliterated this first act of conscious sin.

Fire and Ice

Bombs fell in Glasgow during the war and, like other areas of the city, Pollokshields bore the scars. It seemed not a little appropriate that the bombsite-wasteground near my school became a place where we confronted other dangers. When the annual bonfire night celebrations took place there, I wonder if people reflected on the unwelcome fires which had no doubt burned there some fifteen years before.

For days before the fifth of November, old furniture, logs and wooden crates were stacked into a huge pyramid to be set alight on Bonfire Night. Once aflame, there was no need for a restraining barrier around the blaze. The heat was skin-ripping and the sight and sound of chunks of wood shifting suddenly within the inferno was terrifying. But the ruddy glow lit up the sky and cheered the wintry world.

You didn't even need to have your own fireworks to enjoy the night. People set off their *Roman Candles*, *Golden Rains* and *Silver Fountains* for all to enjoy. Most families had some sparklers and roguish lads delighted in throwing bangers and *Jumping Jacks* behind guileless girls. It was just a harmless evening's entertainment, really.

When our school playground puddles turned to ice and

we slid recklessly over them, we knew it was time to visit that same wasteground for its other amenity. A great river of ice swept down the rough, sloping bank into the flatter area of the site. Late into the evening, children could be seen queuing up to career wildly down this impromptu ice rink. I joined in as willingly as the rest though I was not brave on the ice. Instead of focussing on keeping my balance, I became distracted by imagining what might happen if I fell. Predictably, my thoughts became reality; my tumbled body sped to the end of the slide and my head struck a frozen boulder.

'I came to' – as they say – to face a crowd of anxious faces and a barrage of inexplicable questions.

'What's your name?' my friends demanded.

'Do you know what year it is?'

'How many fingers am I holding up?'

'What's your address?'

My head hurt from the collision – but not nearly as much as it did from the concern of my friends.

If wishes were horses

My family bore my horse phase with mocking good humour. My toddler sobs at not being able to join Wellington on his fine steed in front of the Stirling Library (now the Gallery of Modern Art) were part of family folklore.

In company with JK Rowling, my most favourite book was *The Little White Horse* by Elizabeth Goudge. The little white horse was actually a little white unicorn. The book was a tale of dreams and memories, of love broken and love mended. The ethereal little horse was more of a symbol than a heaving mass of rippling flesh. But I was consumed by the 'horse-ness' of it anyway.

It was when I read *Wish for a Pony* by Monica Edwards that I began to see a real live horse as a real live possibility. The thing was that the perfect stable for 'a great black beast with a white star blazing on its forehead' was in our back green. Next to the line of coal bunkers stood the disused brick-built wash-house. It was MADE for a horse, roomy and dry and close at hand. It was MEANT for a horse. There was conclusive evidence. It had a split door just like a stable so that the horse could put his dear head out to sniff the air while he surveyed his kingdom.

Some of my schoolfriends shared my equine passion.

There were four windows in the wall at the end of the drill-hall facing out onto a secluded part of the school playground. The space between this wall and the playground railings was where we stabled our horses, each tethered in front of a window while we were in class. At break, we rushed to release our steeds who were pawing the ground in anticipation. We mounted, we held up our left hands to grip the reins. With our right hands free to whack our bottoms, we urged our chargers forward through the games of other children.

Fine judgement

My parents were wary about who I kept company with and whose houses I visited. Why was it that the most intriguing friends were deemed the least suitable? Christine came to live in our street and we hit it off right away. We played in the street and in my house but I was not allowed to visit her home. Much later, I discovered Christine's mother was not married to the man she lived with and he was not Christine's father. Evidently I was in mortal danger.

Actually I was quite familiar with the inside of Christine's home – and with Christine's mother and her man. They were very welcoming, and the standards of behaviour expected in their house were much the same as in those of any other family I visited. My decision to overrule my parents' injunction was not uncommon. I'm afraid that when I felt they were being unreasonable, I sometimes assumed the right to choose whether or not to comply.

So it was not unknown for me, at nine or ten years old, to accompany my friend-of-the-day to her home in Mosspark or beyond (a 20-minute bus trip at least) on my way home from school. Strangely, I discovered that other people's parents considered this unreasonable behaviour on *my* part. I would be returned summarily to the bus by a concerned mother at one end to an irate mother at the other.

Susan was a new girl in my class and, on her first day, I walked her home. We chatted outside her close for a while until she invited me in. I was doubtful. My parents didn't even know this girl. Vetting would be necessary before I could visit legally. Susan was pressing. I was weak. *Just for a few minutes*, I promised myself.

The front door was unlocked. We walked in and Susan called out to tell her mother that she was home. 'You go in there,' she pointed to the front room door, 'while I go to the bathroom.'

I opened the front room door to a flurry of frantically flailing bodies. A tousled woman was getting up from the couch, buttoning her blouse feverishly and incorrectly. A rumpled man half lay on the couch. 'Who on earth are you?' the woman demanded, with more than a hint of belligerence and some words that I didn't let my ears hear. I explained that I was her daughter's classmate.

The information was not well-received. I was not well-received. I was gone before Susan returned from the bathroom.

Perhaps my parents had a point.

The Silence Of The Lines

L ining up in the playground took place before each entry
into the school building. Teachers and prefects patrolled
the lines until the silence reached an acceptable pitch for us to
be permitted to walk the hallowed corridors. Ever a chatterer,
I was caught assaulting the silence towards the end of Primary
Five. Mrs Stirling apprehended me.

In her mid 50's, Mrs Stirling was a fine figure of a woman
– a veritable Boudicca with a voice that would certainly have
stirred the ancient Britons to deeds of valour. Mrs Stirling
wore dresses, not skirts and tops like the other teachers. Her
dresses invariably scooped in a generous square down her
front to disclose a mass of uncovered bosom divided by a
deep, deep crevice. Grey curls topped a huge florid face and
that face ended in the sort of chin which demonstrated the
sort of determination required to quell the mindless prattle
of little girls.

I was terrified, horrified, stupefied; terrified because the
face which was thrust down to my level, and the voice which
emitted from it, were vast and angry; horrified, because I
usually kept out of trouble, if only by the skin of my teeth; and
stupefied, because the terror and horror rendered me unable
to think, let alone answer the Gorgon before me.

Each June we waited with interest to be told who our teacher for the following school year would be. When it was announced that Mrs Stirling was to be my next teacher, I announced to my parents that I WOULD HAVE TO BE moved to another school. They laughed mercilessly. But those eight glorious weeks of summer holiday were blighted for me by the prospect of facing Mrs Stirling in the classroom every day for the coming year.

Mrs Stirling taught me for the next two years, the remainder of my primary school life. She shouted, she was not fair, her methods were harsh, but she had an enormous laugh, an enormous personality, an enormous heart and I learned like never before or since.

Under the spell

O n Fridays, Mrs Stirling held The Spelling Bee. The rules were simple. There were two aisles in the classroom between the three columns of desks. One half of the class lined up in each aisle and Mrs Stirling fired spelling words at each of us in turn. If you spelled your word correctly, you stayed where you were. If you were wrong, you went to the end of the line at the front of the classroom. The more words you spelled correctly, the nearer to the back of the room you got. Though it may not have been the point of the exercise, the back of the room was a good place to be. Thick hot water pipes ran round the walls – it was an enviably warm place to be standing.

Mrs Stirling had built up a list of all the sorts of words which people go on spelling wrongly for the rest of their lives if they don't learn them correctly when they are ten years old. There was s-i-e-g-e and s-e-i-z-e; there was n-e-c-e-s-s-a-r-y; there was o-c-c-a-s-i-o-n; there was r-h-y-t-h-m… There were over 250 words in the list. Seldom do I pen a paragraph without making use of a word on Mrs Stirling's list.

It was hot at the back of the classroom beside the pipes and I was on fire with my spelling prowess. The heat was threatening to overcome me but I couldn't make a mistake. I felt close to fainting but I must spell the words correctly. I could not, would not face the walk of shame to the front of the class. My head ached, my eyes ached, my very brain ached. I sank down onto the desk behind me. Only then did Mrs Stirling notice my plight. I was sent home. In acute pain, I was put to bed with a hot water bottle on my pillow.

It seemed I had s-i-n-u-s-i-t-i-s.

Teacher's pet?

W as I the teacher's pet? Certainly there were mutterings to that effect from some of my classmates. In fact I was more like an unpaid classroom assistant in an era when there was no such thing as a paid one. Teachers were responsible for everything from the lowly duties of supervising shoelace-tying and coat-buttoning to the loftier task of broadening and inspiring inquiring young minds.

During the two years that I was in Mrs Stirling's class, she devolved many menial chores to me. I ran errands within and without the school; I tidied the classroom cupboards; I wrote sums up on the board; I handed out jotters; I sharpened pencils; in short, I was a general dogsbody.

I have a particularly clear recall of one Friday afternoon when Mrs Stirling was busy completing our report cards. The class was enjoying an unusually relaxed afternoon, reading their library books. As our teacher finished filling in each card, she would summon me to add up the pupil's marks to produce a total out of 250. Handling every report card meant that I was privy not only to my classmates' marks, but to any comments made by Mrs Stirling about them. Clearly, privacy was of less concern than getting the job done.

Wearily, I trudged back and forth for each bout of

calculation, too timid to tell her that I was feeling rather unwell. That was an unfortunate omission. There came a moment when an unstoppable tide of sickness overcame me, and I deposited my partially digested lunch on the floor of the classroom. The janitor was sent for and arrived bearing sawdust to soak up the moisture, as well as an outsize broom and shovel to remove the offensive matter; my classmates were treated to an extra playtime; I was sent off to walk to the sanctuary of my home; and Mrs Stirling was left to do her own addition.

If it was the *teacher* who was inconsiderate enough to be unwell, there was no provision for a deputy to stand in. Sometimes the headmaster would put aside the larger concerns of running the school and take a class. More often, we were divided up amongst other classes – three or four of us squeezing into a desk for two – and set to do the work of that class, whatever its level.

For a short spell, Mrs Stirling had a medical condition which required weekly hospital appointments during school hours. Exercising her creativity as to how to deal with her 33 pupils while she was away, she hit on a novel idea. While she attended the clinic, I attended to the class. I ensured that her instructions for the morning's lessons were carried out quietly and efficiently. The teacher next door would pop in from time to time to check all was well. I corrected sums, revised spelling, parsed sentences and read out history questions until Mrs Stirling arrived and donned her iron glove.

If being 'teacher's drudge' makes you 'teacher's pet', then that's what I was. But if that honour is supposed to come with special privileges, then I must protest.

Mrs Stirling had high standards for our written work.

Despite my best intentions and ferocious efforts, the appearance of my written work remained a disappointment to her – and to me. I began each new jotter with high expectations and a careful pen; predictably, hope was blotted out by the time I turned the first page.

Each week we wrote in our 'ink exercise' jotters. No matter how assiduous I was in copying from my rough draft, my hand and brain seemed unable to cooperate with one another. Week after week, I faced the same insoluble dilemma. What should I do when I made a mistake in the ink exercise?

I still don't know the answer. We were not allowed to score out, tippex had not yet been invented, and ink-rubbers tended to remove the paper as well as the error. My solution was to write the correct word over the incorrect one; my hope was that one would blend seamlessly into the other. It seemed simple enough but I found that, like a home-cut fringe, the more I did, the worse it looked. 'One more snip here should do it,' the would-be hairdresser mutters. In just such a hopeful tone, the errant pen-wielder adds yet another stroke in a vain bid to conceal the erroneous word beneath.

This most monstrous of crimes – called 'Changing' by Mrs Stirling – was an offence deserving the harshest punishment. Faithful aide I might be, but more than once, my practice of 'Changing' brought the full weight of Mrs Stirling's belt down on my helpful little hand.

Street dancing

A ndrew came from Canada to my school in Primary Six. We were best friends from his very first day there, when I was detailed by Mrs Stirling to see him home in case he got lost. Andrew came attached to liberal young parents and five younger siblings – quite the reverse of me with my three older brothers and much older parents for whom the word *liberal*, unless applied to a political party, paved the road to Hell.

I spent many hours in Andrew's house and found that, despite his parents' free and easy ways, things got done, proper food was eaten, children were cleaned and taught to be polite, and everybody seemed to have fun.

Was it part of the general *joie de vivre* which Andrew and I felt in those carefree days that we saw fit to demonstrate *The Mrs Mcleod* (the new country dance we'd learned at school) in the main shopping street? Certainly our *joie* was lost on at least two observers who felt impelled to inform the school of our shocking behaviour. Not hard to identify the culprits: only eight were in the country dance team, only two were inseparable, only one had pigtails.

When I took my sums out to be marked by my teacher, next day, I think I could detect just the glimmer of a twinkle behind Mrs Stirling's admonishing exterior as she bade us curb our enthusiasm and confine our dancing to the drill-hall.

Hell hath no fury

Andrew was a year older than I was. I was actually nearer in age to his younger sister, Maggie, and the three of us got on together famously. We played Snakes and ladders, Monopoly, card games (sshh, don't tell my parents) and generally larked around.

Inevitably, we reached the stage of playing 'Dares'. Inevitably, the dares became more daring. Inevitably, they involved removing bits of clothing. Inevitably, Andrew wanted us to show him our knickers. Perhaps because there were two of us, we did. Inevitably, he wanted us to pull down our knickers. Hmmm, we were less sure about this. We all three went into the bathroom in their house. We seemed to think this location less likely to arouse parental questioning. After some haggling, it was agreed that we would pull our knickers down very swiftly and straight back up, ON CONDITION that Andrew would reciprocate straight after.

Oh Andrew, do you ever look back on that day and reflect on how much more dignified it would have been if you had kept your side of the bargain?

As it was, no amount of your earnest protestations were a match for the four hands and the combined strength of two indignant lassies.

Hanging out the dirty washing

Monday was our mother's day at the Steamie. Being keen on 'clean', this was a highlight of the week even though it involved piling the washing for a family of six into a wooden bogey on old pram wheels and pushing it well over half a mile to the washhouse. Worse still, the journey back with the heavy wet load was all uphill. But she always relished this weekly venture and talked of it fondly – almost boastfully.

When I went with her in the school holidays, I could see why she liked it so much. Not only did she have company while working at heavy, tedious tasks – with willing hands to help fold sheets, and a host of advice on all topics – but what company it was! It was friendly, it was cheery, it was bawdy, it was a lark a minute – and not a man in sight!

Monday was not a morning to tarry in your bed unless you wanted the sheets snatched from about you. No husband, child or cat was left unturned in the great hunt for dirty washing to fuel this morning of social abandon.

I had a new turquoise cardigan. Unusually, I was the *first* owner of this cardigan. I cannot deny that as the only girl, relations and friends of the family favoured me financially. It really wasn't my fault that my maiden aunts saw fit to send

£1 for my brother's birthday with instructions that 15 shillings of it was to be spent on me. A future oft-quoted cry went up that day from my hard-done-by brother. '15 shillings for a doll for her and 5 shillings for me – and it's MY birthday.'

One elderly gentleman, an adherent of the *Hebrew Christian Alliance*, made it his habit to mark my birthday with a guinea. Yes, a guinea – or 21 shillings, if you want to be modern. That same gentleman gave me a fine violin. I delighted in using it at school and casually showing the label stuck in its belly. It purported, along with many thousands of others no doubt, to have been made in Cremona in 1711 by the great Stradivarius.

But I digress from the turquoise cardigan which I bought with that magnificent guinea. I wore it on Saturday just for the fun of it and I wore it on Sunday to brighten the day's tedious sandwich of Church, Sunday School, Church. I felt so well-dressed. Oh, I loved the turquoise cardigan.

Being light-coloured, my cardigan showed all the marks of two days' wear. It was the first item to be dispatched to the bogey for the weekly wash. But I could not bear to be parted from it. I retrieved it from its ignominious juxtaposition to the week's used hankies and determined to wear it to school. Be assured, there was no maternal awareness of, never mind agreement to, this action. In fact, the matter had been discussed on Sunday night and my treasure consigned to the dirty washing there and then.

It was my last year in primary school and I was school captain. The responsibility was heavy. It involved patrolling the lines in the playground or standing at strategic points on the stairs inside the school to detain any pupil daring to talk en route to class. I was on indoor duty that day and my less than pristine cardigan (in non-school colours) was on full display to our glamorous and disdainful headmistress. I was no favourite of hers; she seemed not a little triumphant to call me to her office to tear strips off me for coming to school in dirty clothes. She ended her harangue by warning me that were I to fail again to set a good example, I would be DISBADGED.

I'm not sure why I divulged this to my mother. I could see that it caused her a painful mix of shame and triumph.

I still loved the turquoise cardigan.

Fruity dilemma

C ould you pop into Templeton's on your way back to school, please?' Mrs Stirling asked one day. 'I'd like some apples. Get me five Cox's Orange Pippins.'

I'd never heard of Cox's Orange Pippins. I repeated the name over and over as I walked. The more I said it, the stranger it sounded. How could apples be orange? Perhaps it was a slip of the tongue and really she wanted oranges, not apples. Perhaps she wanted oranges *and* apples? Maybe she didn't say 'apple' at all. She definitely said the word 'orange'. So that's what I went for.

Mrs Stirling was gracious to me, though she had a funny look on her face and a bit of a twitch when I handed her the fruit. I bet she couldn't wait to get to the staffroom.

Defender of the realm

It was around Primary Six that the first stirrings of knowledge that boys and girls are different enlivened our lives. Separate school playgrounds for boys and girls meant that the journeys to and from school were the stage on which we played out our first encounters.

If you are hoping to read of fumblings in the back close and stolen kisses in the park, you might as well stop reading now. The relationship between the boys and the girls became that of hunters and hunted. Where before we had walked home contentedly chatting in mixed groups, now the chase was on. Every journey home from school entailed little gaggles of girls running between closes, squealing, giggling, and looking over their shoulders for the posse of boys who would inevitably appear and attempt to catch hold of a girl, any girl and... well, actually I don't know what. The thrill was all in the pursuit.

I was small – but I was fast, I was strong and I daily faced up to three older brothers. It became my mission in life to protect my more delicate, more feminine friends from the attentions of those rough, tough lads. I would herd my charges to the safety of one close and then fly out at the marauders, beating them off with my hands, feet, and maybe nails too, while the girls ran past to the next sanctuary.

I gained quite a reputation for fighting and I gloried in it. Not even the ripping of my school skirt from hem to waist as I climbed some railings to further my advance could dampen my zeal. It was a ludicrously forlorn hope that the state of my skirt would go unnoticed by my mother though I hopefully put it out for washing without a word. But even the ensuing row at home didn't stop me fighting. I did, of course, protect my parents from the real reason for my torn apparel.

Billy Campbell was a fierce assailant; he and I enjoyed many a spat. Enlisting support from a watching crowd, he detailed another boy to grab me from behind, and grip my arms at the elbows so that I was unable to get my hands on my adversary. With a massive effort of will more than strength, I jerked myself forward out of my jailer's grasp. The force projected me head first towards the taunting face of Billy. Our heads collided and I learned that 'seeing stars' is not just a picturesque phrase. Each of us sported what the adults called 'a pigeon's egg' on our foreheads. I fobbed my parents off with the old 'walked into a wall' story. Our teacher who saw Billy's matching lump knew the truth.

Maybe it knocked some sense into me…

A bit of a sing-along

My mother told me that, when she was twelve years old, she took part in a school show. By then she had grown to her full height of 4 foot 11½ inches and, for a brief time, was almost as round as she was tall. Having a fine singing voice, it was obvious that she should be given a solo part. Sadly the powers-that-were decided that she sounded very much better than she looked. She was cast as 'The Moon' and made to sing behind a screen.

In my school, it was also the custom for the Primary Seven classes to prepare a show for the delight of their parents and the rest of the school. It was performed in the drill-hall, half of which became the stage. The rest of the school watched the performance sitting cross-legged on the floor.

I must have been about eight years old the year that *Cinderella* was the chosen piece. No doubt the carriage bearing the heroine to the ball was a wooden desk covered in orange crêpe paper, but I know I saw the beautiful princess stepping daintily into her pumpkin conveyance, and I dreamt of it long after. I couldn't wait for it to be our turn to create such a magical spectacle.

And indeed, the day arrived when, as the oldest children

in the school, it was our turn to mount a production. Our show was to be *Snow White* and it was a little operetta. Playing in to my hands, I thought. Acting was maybe not my strongest suit, but singing! Why, everybody knew I sang all the time, anything, anywhere. The lead role was mine without a doubt.

Mr Bell, a music teacher from the 'Big School', came to our school weekly to play the piano while we sang such rousing numbers as *Early one morning, Ho ro my nut-brown maiden, Sir Eglamore that valiant knight*. He and our class teacher conferred over the show casting and announced their decisions. Lanky, red-haired Maureen was the wicked stepmother. Good choice, I conceded. The tall, well-favoured Gordon was to be the prince. Excellent decision. The lovely Carol of the ringlets was to be Snow White. I was incredulous as much as devastated. Pretty, Carol may have been, but she was no singer.

But wait, our teacher had more to say. It seemed that Mr Bell would not be coming for a few weeks and anyway once a week visits would not be nearly enough for us to learn the whole show. So they had hatched a plan. It seemed that I – yes you, Esther Cohen, that's right – was to learn to play and sing the whole show and teach the songs to my class mates. Hmmm. Now I saw why I had been 'overlooked' for the part of Snow White. I was needed elsewhere. Hmmm. I was torn between pride at being assigned this task and disappointment at being denied the glory of treading the boards.

Dutifully, I took the score home, learned to sing and play all the songs, and taught them to my classmates. Mr Bell was pleased with our efforts. In fact, he went so far as to declare that I should play for the actual performances. So I did.

In my mind, it became *my* show. I was desperate for it to be a success. But to my critical ears, the solo singers just weren't up to it. They couldn't be heard well enough and I feared that the audience would not be enchanted and beguiled by the spectacle.

I was behind the piano. Perhaps it was a memory of my mother singing behind a screen that gave me the idea of singing along with every soloist to amplify the sound. Anyway, that is what I did.

I can scarcely bear to think about it, let alone write about it. But there – I've said it now.

Cross-talk

I won't forget the night of the fourth of September 1962.
I was very late home from my piano lesson.

Where on earth have you been? It's pitch-dark. I've been worried to death. And you're absolutely drenched. What on earth have you been up to?'

'I'm sorry Mummy. I was coming along Darnley Street and I saw all these people. Hundreds of people and—'

'For goodness sake, look at your coat. It's soaked right through. Take it off, quick. I'll need to put it up on the pulley.'

'But all these people, Mummy, they were standing all along Albert Drive, you know beside the tram depot there and—'

'You're absolutely soaked to the skin. Get those wet things off quick before you catch your death. Go and get your nightie, quick.'

'And then lots of trams started coming in from Eglinton Street, Mummy. I wasn't going to stay but they all were going into the depot and some of them were really old and—'

'Just look at the state of your hair. It's absolutely dripping. Undo your plaits, quick. Here's a towel. Now sit there in front of the fire. Oh I just hope you don't get a chill.'

'And somebody told me that the trams were never coming out again and—'

'Oh for goodness sake, you were out in all that rain in your new shoes! They'll be ruined. They're absolutely sodden. Get them off quick so I can stuff them with paper.'

'And people were crying and putting pennies down on the tramlines and then picking them up after the trams had passed and the pennies were bent and—'

'For heaven's sake, look at your good socks. What on earth's happened to your feet? Is that blood?'

The red insoles in my new shoes had dissolved into a ruddy mush. My white socks were indelibly red.

I'm glad I was late home from my piano lesson.
I won't forget the night of the fourth of September 1962.

Rite of passage

The 'Qualy Dance'* took place in the last days of our last term in primary school. In the playground, we had talked of nothing else for weeks. On the day itself, Andrew announced that he was going to collect me from my house and escort me there. Apprehensive does not begin to describe my feelings at his declaration. Although Andrew and I spent a lot of time together, our friendship wasn't anything I ever talked about at home. Why would I? We were having harmless fun together but that was not how my parents would have viewed it. So on that evening, I followed the pattern of communication by which I managed most of my family life; I said nothing at all and let matters take their course:

> *Today is a day for letting my hair down. Literally. My pigtails are to be freed and my hair will cascade in soft waves down the back of my sparkly, midnight blue, net-covered, magical, if hand-me-down, dress. Except that*

---

*Primary Seven, the last year of primary school, was also called the 'Qualifying Class'. During that year, we sat our eleven-plus exam which determined which secondary school we were considered 'qualified' to attend.

my hair is straight – unequivocally, unmistakably straight. Well, not if it gets wet and then gets dried in tight pigtails. Then it becomes gloriously kinked and as rippled as any sea.

An inner voice whispers, Well that's what to do then. Get in the bath, get your hair wet, get your hair dry and then you'll have your ripples.

And that is what I do. I jump in the bath and give my hair a thorough soaking.

That inner voice didn't have much brain. It's easy enough to wet my hair, but drying it is another matter. What wouldn't I give for a hair dryer! Despite my mother's vigorous towelling, my hair remains both wet and straight.

It'll just have to be pigtails then. My mother has a tiny brainwave. She doubles up my plaits so that the bows, which match my dress (did I mention my midnight blue, sparkly... oh sorry, I won't go on about it even though it is so magical), nestle behind my ears. They look quite cute though I am a little downcast about the lack of flowing locks – not least because I know that their absence is my own fault.

My stomach is churning.

Any minute now, they'll find out about Andrew and it won't matter about my plaits, my ribbons or my sparkly dress as I won't be allowed to go.

[Doorbell rings]

MOTHER: Who can that be?

ME [*small voice*]: It's for me.

MOTHER: For you? Who is it? Is Margaret walking up with you?

ME [smaller voice]: No.

MOTHER: Well who is it then?

ME [*even smaller voice*]: It's a boy.

MOTHER: A boy? A boy! Quickly, Daddy! Go and open the door!

And it is a boy. A beaming boy with his fair hair slicked down and wearing... a kilt. Amazingly, my parents smile. In fact, they laugh. A boy has come to take their little girl to the school dance. Such a thing has never happened anywhere in the world before! They send us off with their good humour lightening our hearts.

At the end of the day...

Family prayers often took place round the kitchen table after our evening meal. My father read many of them from a little book. Usually, in our Baptist church, prayers were improvised, not read. It seemed to me that anyone who had to write out a prayer before delivering it was considered to be faintly suspect. The 'truly devout' just opened their mouths and let the words flow. In retrospect, a few more written-out prayers might have been quite welcome; some of the speakers clearly felt it their duty to give a resumé of all the doctrines they espoused – and there were many.

It wasn't until I attended an Episcopal Church later on in life that I realised that my father was reading from the *Book of Common Prayer* and that the words we dutifully repeated after him were being spoken all over the world. That was a welcome moment of connection for me; no one else I knew took part in family prayers.

Sometimes our day would end with prayer, but more often we sang:

> *Lord keep us safe this night*
> *Secure from all our fears.*
> *May angels guard us while we sleep*
> *Till morning light appears.*

My father had a strong voice but he could only sing the tune, unadorned. He led the singing and we all joined him. I imagine that when the family first sang this gentle verse, we all sang the tune with him, except for my mother who could harmonise any song. In time, each of us children found that we too could embellish and complement the melody.

So by the end of our childhood, we often sang in six separate parts – all in harmony. It touched deep. Now, it seems like a metaphor for our family life. When we were young, our father dictated the way we should live our lives. Later, with our differing natures, we each adopted our own routes, weaving around his straight and narrow road – not completely in harmony with the tune he sang, but not wholly in discord either.

The last time we sang that verse was when I was sixteen. We were standing round my father's hospital bed not long before he died.

Keep us Safe this Night

Words: John Leland

Tune: Beethoven

Arr: E. Cohen

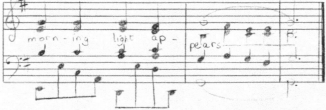

Lord, keep us safe this night, se-cure from all four fears. May angels guard us while we sleep till morning light appears.

Thanks. . .

Putting this book together has been a mostly a family affair although the first person to read a draft was my friend, Denise Steele. Her rather unenviable task was to tell me whether she thought my stories would be of interest to more people than my nearest and dearest. Gosh, I hope she was right!

On the dedication page, I mention a sketch which my children delivered on my Silver Wedding Anniversary. It highlighted some of the elements which make a 1950s childhood so different from a present-day one, albeit carried to ridiculous excess. Complete with appropriate (and inappropriate!) accents, it left me and my husband weak with laughter. Well done to Tim who came up with the idea. It jumpstarted me into writing down all the snippets of stories I had been telling the family for years if for no other reason than to ensure their veracity for posterity. Left only in the imaginative minds of my children, I could see my tales would very quickly be distorted into grotesque caricatures.

Thanks to Chris for writing such an insightful blurb, to Miriam for her lovely cat-clef symbol, and to Lewis who did the proof reading with an eagle eye. It has been cheering to see their enthusiasm for this venture.

Of course there can be no show without Punch – in this case, my husband, Archie, who has considered every *smart quote*, *endash*, *drop cap* and much more besides. He may not quite have wielded Punch's big stick but he has kept me at it relentlessly and driven himself along with me.

What on earth will we talk about now it's finished?

Esther Cohen, 10 April 2016